# 50 Latin American Dinner Recipes for Home

By: Kelly Johnson

# Table of Contents

- Arepas
- Arroz con Pollo
- Asado
- Bandeja Paisa
- Bolon de Verde
- Burritos
- Ceviche
- Chicharrón
- Chile Relleno
- Chimichurri Steak
- Churrasco
- Cochinita Pibil
- Empanadas
- Enchiladas
- Feijoada
- Flautas
- Gallo Pinto
- Hallacas
- Huevos Rancheros
- Lomo Saltado
- Mofongo
- Moqueca
- Pabellón Criollo
- Pastel de Choclo
- Pastelitos
- Patacones
- Pernil
- Picadillo
- Picanha
- Pisco Sour
- Pão de Queijo
- Quesadillas
- Ropa Vieja
- Sancocho
- Seco de Pollo

- Shrimp Tacos
- Sopes
- Tacos al Pastor
- Tamales
- Tostones
- Tortilla Soup
- Vaca Frita
- Yuca Frita
- Ajiaco
- Birria Tacos
- Carne Asada
- Chilaquiles
- Chupe de Camarones
- Ensalada Rusa
- Pollo a la Brasa

## Arepas

Ingredients

- 2 cups of pre-cooked white cornmeal (Harina PAN or similar)
- 2 1/2 cups of warm water
- 1 teaspoon of salt
- 1 tablespoon of vegetable oil (for cooking)

Instructions

1. Mix Dough:
   - In a large bowl, combine the warm water and salt.
   - Gradually add the cornmeal to the water while mixing with your hands until a dough forms.
   - Let the dough rest for about 5 minutes to allow the cornmeal to absorb the water fully.
2. Form Arepas:
   - Divide the dough into equal-sized balls (about the size of a golf ball).
   - Flatten each ball gently with your hands to form a disc about 1/2 inch thick.
3. Cook Arepas:
   - Heat a large non-stick skillet or griddle over medium heat and add a little oil.
   - Place the arepas on the skillet and cook for about 5-7 minutes on each side, until they develop a golden crust.
   - Optionally, you can finish cooking them in a preheated oven at 350°F (175°C) for 10-15 minutes to ensure they are cooked through.
4. Serve:
   - Let the arepas cool slightly before slicing them open.
   - Fill with your favorite fillings, such as cheese, shredded beef, chicken, avocado, or beans.

Enjoy your homemade arepas!

**Arroz con Pollo**

Ingredients

- 2 cups of long-grain rice
- 4 chicken thighs (bone-in, skin-on)
- 1 onion, chopped
- 1 bell pepper, chopped
- 2 cloves of garlic, minced
- 1 cup of peas
- 1 cup of diced tomatoes (fresh or canned)
- 3 cups of chicken broth
- 1/2 cup of dry white wine (optional)
- 1 teaspoon of ground cumin
- 1 teaspoon of paprika
- 1/2 teaspoon of turmeric or saffron threads
- 1 bay leaf
- 2 tablespoons of olive oil
- Salt and pepper to taste
- Fresh cilantro or parsley for garnish
- Lime wedges for serving (optional)

Instructions

1. Prepare Chicken:
   - Season the chicken thighs with salt, pepper, and paprika.
   - Heat 1 tablespoon of olive oil in a large skillet or pot over medium-high heat.
   - Brown the chicken thighs on both sides, about 5-7 minutes per side, then remove from the skillet and set aside.
2. Cook Vegetables:
   - In the same skillet, add the remaining tablespoon of olive oil.
   - Add the chopped onion, bell pepper, and minced garlic. Cook until the vegetables are softened, about 5 minutes.
3. Add Rice and Spices:
   - Stir in the rice, cumin, turmeric (or saffron), and bay leaf. Cook for 2-3 minutes, stirring frequently, until the rice is lightly toasted.
4. Add Liquids:
   - Pour in the chicken broth and white wine (if using).
   - Add the diced tomatoes and peas, stirring to combine.

- Return the browned chicken thighs to the skillet, nestling them into the rice mixture.
5. **Simmer:**
    - Bring the mixture to a boil, then reduce the heat to low.
    - Cover the skillet and let it simmer for about 25-30 minutes, or until the rice is cooked and the chicken is tender.
    - Check occasionally and add more broth if needed to keep the rice from drying out.
6. **Finish and Serve:**
    - Once cooked, remove the skillet from heat and let it sit, covered, for an additional 5 minutes.
    - Fluff the rice with a fork and garnish with fresh cilantro or parsley.
    - Serve with lime wedges on the side, if desired.

Enjoy your delicious Arroz con Pollo!

## Asado

Ingredients

- 2 lbs (900 g) of beef ribs or short ribs
- 2 lbs (900 g) of pork ribs
- 2 lbs (900 g) of chorizo sausages
- 2 lbs (900 g) of chicken thighs or drumsticks
- 1/4 cup of coarse salt
- 1/4 cup of chimichurri sauce (optional)

Instructions

1. Prepare the Grill:
    - Preheat your grill to a medium-high heat. If using charcoal, allow the coals to burn until they are covered with a white ash.
2. Season the Meat:
    - Generously sprinkle coarse salt over all sides of the beef and pork ribs, chorizo, and chicken pieces. The coarse salt helps to form a crust on the meat while it grills.
3. Grill the Meat:
    - Place the beef and pork ribs on the grill, bone side down. Cook for about 1-1.5 hours, turning occasionally, until the meat is tender and has a nice char.
    - Add the chorizo sausages to the grill. Cook for about 15-20 minutes, turning occasionally, until they are cooked through and browned.
    - Add the chicken thighs or drumsticks to the grill. Cook for about 30-40 minutes, turning occasionally, until they are cooked through and have a crispy skin.
4. Serve:
    - Remove the meat from the grill and let it rest for a few minutes before serving.
    - Optionally, serve with chimichurri sauce on the side for added flavor.

Enjoy your traditional Asado!

**Bandeja Paisa**

Ingredients

- For the Beans:
    - 2 cups of red kidney beans, soaked overnight
    - 1 onion, chopped
    - 2 cloves of garlic, minced
    - 1 tomato, chopped
    - 1 tablespoon of vegetable oil
    - 1 teaspoon of ground cumin
    - 1 teaspoon of salt
    - 1 bay leaf
    - 6 cups of water
- For the Rice:
    - 2 cups of long-grain white rice
    - 4 cups of water
    - 1 tablespoon of vegetable oil
    - 1 teaspoon of salt
- For the Meat:
    - 1 lb of ground beef
    - 1 onion, chopped
    - 1 tomato, chopped
    - 2 cloves of garlic, minced
    - 1 tablespoon of vegetable oil
    - 1 teaspoon of ground cumin
    - Salt and pepper to taste
- For the Pork Belly:
    - 1 lb of pork belly, cut into strips
    - Salt to taste
- For the Plantains:
    - 2 ripe plantains, peeled and sliced
    - Vegetable oil for frying
- Other Ingredients:
    - 4 eggs
    - 4 chorizo sausages
    - 2 avocados, sliced
    - 4 arepas
    - Lime wedges for serving

Instructions

1. Cook the Beans:
   - In a large pot, heat the vegetable oil over medium heat.
   - Add the chopped onion and garlic, cooking until softened.
   - Add the chopped tomato, cumin, and salt, stirring to combine.
   - Add the soaked beans, water, and bay leaf.
   - Bring to a boil, then reduce heat and simmer for 1.5 to 2 hours, or until the beans are tender.
2. Cook the Rice:
   - In a medium pot, bring the water to a boil.
   - Add the rice, vegetable oil, and salt.
   - Reduce the heat to low, cover, and simmer for 20 minutes or until the rice is cooked and water is absorbed.
3. Prepare the Ground Beef:
   - In a skillet, heat the vegetable oil over medium heat.
   - Add the chopped onion and garlic, cooking until softened.
   - Add the ground beef, breaking it up with a spoon.
   - Add the chopped tomato, cumin, salt, and pepper.
   - Cook until the beef is browned and cooked through.
4. Fry the Pork Belly:
   - Season the pork belly strips with salt.
   - In a large skillet, cook the pork belly over medium heat until crispy and golden brown.
   - Remove from skillet and drain on paper towels.
5. Fry the Plantains:
   - In a deep skillet or frying pan, heat the vegetable oil over medium heat.
   - Fry the plantain slices until golden brown and caramelized.
   - Remove and drain on paper towels.
6. Cook the Chorizo and Eggs:
   - In the same skillet, cook the chorizo sausages until browned and cooked through.
   - In another pan, fry the eggs sunny side up.
7. Assemble the Bandeja Paisa:
   - On a large plate, arrange a portion of rice, a serving of beans, and a portion of ground beef.
   - Add a few strips of pork belly, a chorizo sausage, and a fried egg.
   - Add a few slices of fried plantain and avocado.
   - Place an arepa on the side.

- Serve with lime wedges for squeezing over the dish.

Enjoy your hearty and delicious Bandeja Paisa!

## Bolon de Verde

Ingredients

- 4 green plantains (plátanos verdes)
- 1 cup of crumbled queso fresco (or any fresh cheese like feta)
- 1 cup of cooked and crumbled chicharrón (pork cracklings) or bacon
- 3 tablespoons of butter or lard
- Salt to taste
- Vegetable oil for frying

Instructions

1. Prepare the Plantains:
    - Peel the plantains and cut them into chunks.
    - Bring a pot of salted water to a boil. Add the plantain chunks and cook for about 15-20 minutes, or until they are tender but still firm.
2. Mash the Plantains:
    - Drain the cooked plantains and let them cool slightly.
    - In a large bowl, mash the plantains while they are still warm. Add the butter or lard and mix until well combined. Season with salt to taste.
3. Form the Bolones:
    - Take a handful of the mashed plantain mixture and flatten it slightly in your hand.
    - Place a spoonful of crumbled cheese and crumbled chicharrón or bacon in the center.
    - Carefully fold the plantain mixture around the filling and shape it into a ball. Repeat until all the mixture is used.
4. Fry the Bolones:
    - In a deep skillet, heat about an inch of vegetable oil over medium heat.
    - Fry the plantain balls in batches until they are golden brown and crispy on all sides, about 3-5 minutes per batch.
    - Remove and drain on paper towels.
5. Serve:
    - Serve the bolones de verde hot, with a side of aji sauce or your favorite dipping sauce.

Enjoy your Bolon de Verde!

# Burritos

Ingredients

- For the Filling:
    - 1 lb (450 g) of ground beef or chicken
    - 1 onion, chopped
    - 2 cloves of garlic, minced
    - 1 bell pepper, chopped
    - 1 can (15 oz) of black beans, drained and rinsed
    - 1 cup of cooked rice
    - 1 cup of corn kernels (fresh or frozen)
    - 1 can (10 oz) of diced tomatoes with green chilies
    - 2 tablespoons of taco seasoning
    - 1/2 teaspoon of salt
    - 1/4 teaspoon of black pepper
    - 2 tablespoons of vegetable oil
- For Assembly:
    - 8 large flour tortillas
    - 1 cup of shredded cheddar cheese
    - 1 cup of shredded lettuce
    - 1/2 cup of sour cream
    - 1/2 cup of salsa
    - 1/4 cup of chopped cilantro
    - Lime wedges (optional)

Instructions

1. Cook the Filling:
    - Heat the vegetable oil in a large skillet over medium heat.
    - Add the chopped onion and minced garlic, cooking until softened, about 3 minutes.
    - Add the ground beef or chicken to the skillet. Cook until browned and fully cooked through.
    - Stir in the chopped bell pepper and cook for another 2-3 minutes.
    - Add the black beans, cooked rice, corn kernels, diced tomatoes with green chilies, taco seasoning, salt, and black pepper. Mix well and cook for another 5 minutes, until everything is heated through and well combined.
2. Warm the Tortillas:

- Heat the flour tortillas in a dry skillet over medium heat for about 30 seconds on each side, or until they are warm and pliable. Alternatively, you can wrap them in foil and warm them in a preheated oven at 350°F (175°C) for about 10 minutes.
3. Assemble the Burritos:
    - Lay a warm tortilla flat on a clean surface.
    - Spoon a generous amount of the filling mixture onto the center of the tortilla.
    - Sprinkle some shredded cheddar cheese over the filling.
    - Add a handful of shredded lettuce, a dollop of sour cream, and a spoonful of salsa.
    - Sprinkle with chopped cilantro.
    - Fold the sides of the tortilla over the filling, then roll it up from the bottom to the top to form a burrito.
    - Repeat with the remaining tortillas and filling.
4. Serve:
    - Serve the burritos hot, with lime wedges on the side if desired.

Enjoy your delicious homemade burritos!

## Ceviche

Ingredients

- 1 lb (450 g) of fresh fish fillets (such as snapper, sea bass, or halibut), cut into 1/2-inch cubes
- 1 cup of freshly squeezed lime juice (about 8-10 limes)
- 1/2 cup of freshly squeezed lemon juice (about 4-5 lemons)
- 1 small red onion, thinly sliced
- 1 jalapeño pepper, seeded and finely chopped
- 1/2 cup of chopped cilantro
- 1 medium tomato, diced
- 1 cucumber, peeled, seeded, and diced
- 1/2 cup of chopped fresh parsley (optional)
- Salt and pepper to taste
- Tortilla chips or tostadas for serving
- Avocado slices (optional)

Instructions

1. Prepare the Fish:
   - Place the cubed fish in a large glass or ceramic bowl.
2. Marinate the Fish:
   - Pour the lime juice and lemon juice over the fish, ensuring the fish is completely submerged.
   - Cover the bowl with plastic wrap and refrigerate for at least 1 hour, or until the fish is opaque and "cooked" through by the citrus juices. This can take up to 2-3 hours depending on the thickness of the fish pieces.
3. Mix the Vegetables:
   - In a separate bowl, combine the thinly sliced red onion, chopped jalapeño, chopped cilantro, diced tomato, diced cucumber, and chopped parsley (if using).
4. Combine and Season:
   - Once the fish is "cooked" through, drain the excess marinade from the fish.
   - Add the marinated fish to the bowl with the mixed vegetables and gently toss to combine.
   - Season with salt and pepper to taste.
5. Serve:
   - Serve the ceviche chilled, with tortilla chips or tostadas on the side.
   - Optionally, garnish with avocado slices.

Enjoy your fresh and tangy ceviche!

## Chicharrón

Ingredients

- 2 lbs (900 g) of pork belly with skin
- 1 tablespoon of baking soda
- 1 tablespoon of salt
- 4 cups of water (for boiling)
- Vegetable oil for frying

Instructions

1. Prepare the Pork Belly:
    - Rinse the pork belly under cold water and pat it dry with paper towels.
    - Cut the pork belly into 2-inch wide strips.
2. Boil the Pork Belly:
    - In a large pot, combine the water, baking soda, and salt.
    - Add the pork belly strips and bring to a boil over medium-high heat.
    - Reduce the heat to medium and simmer for about 30 minutes, or until the pork belly is tender but not falling apart.
    - Drain the pork belly and pat it dry with paper towels to remove any excess moisture.
3. Dry and Rest the Pork Belly:
    - Place the pork belly strips on a wire rack set over a baking sheet.
    - Let them rest in the refrigerator for at least 1 hour, or up to overnight. This helps to dry out the skin, which will make it crispier when fried.
4. Fry the Pork Belly:
    - In a large, deep skillet or pot, heat about 2 inches of vegetable oil to 350°F (175°C).
    - Carefully add the pork belly strips to the hot oil in batches, being cautious of any splattering.
    - Fry for about 5-7 minutes, or until the skin is golden brown and crispy.
    - Remove the chicharrón from the oil and drain on paper towels.
5. Serve:
    - Let the chicharrón cool slightly before cutting into bite-sized pieces.
    - Serve with lime wedges and hot sauce on the side.

Enjoy your crispy and delicious chicharrón!

**Chile Relleno**

Ingredients

- 6 large poblano peppers
- 1 cup of shredded Monterey Jack cheese
- 1 cup of shredded cheddar cheese
- 1 cup of corn kernels (fresh or frozen)
- 1/2 cup of diced onion
- 2 cloves of garlic, minced
- 1/2 cup of all-purpose flour
- 4 large eggs, separated
- 1 teaspoon of salt
- Vegetable oil for frying
- Red salsa or enchilada sauce for serving
- Fresh cilantro leaves for garnish (optional)

Instructions

1. Roast and Peel the Peppers:
    - Preheat the broiler in your oven.
    - Place the poblano peppers on a baking sheet and broil, turning occasionally, until the skins are charred and blistered all over, about 8-10 minutes.
    - Transfer the roasted peppers to a bowl and cover with plastic wrap. Let them steam for about 10 minutes.
    - Once cooled, peel off the charred skins, then carefully make a slit lengthwise down one side of each pepper and remove the seeds and membranes.
2. Prepare the Filling:
    - In a skillet, heat a tablespoon of vegetable oil over medium heat.
    - Add the diced onion and minced garlic, cooking until softened, about 3 minutes.
    - Add the corn kernels and cook for another 2-3 minutes.
    - Remove from heat and let the mixture cool slightly.
    - In a bowl, mix together the shredded Monterey Jack cheese and shredded cheddar cheese. Add the cooled corn mixture and mix until well combined.
3. Fill the Peppers:
    - Stuff each roasted poblano pepper with the cheese and corn mixture, ensuring they are evenly filled.

4. Prepare the Batter:
   - In a large bowl, beat the egg whites with an electric mixer until stiff peaks form.
   - In a separate bowl, whisk the egg yolks with the flour and salt until smooth.
   - Gently fold the egg yolk mixture into the beaten egg whites until just combined.
5. Fry the Stuffed Peppers:
   - In a large skillet, heat about 1 inch of vegetable oil over medium-high heat until hot but not smoking.
   - Dip each stuffed poblano pepper into the egg batter, coating it evenly.
   - Carefully place the battered peppers in the hot oil, working in batches if necessary.
   - Fry the peppers for about 3-4 minutes on each side, or until they are golden brown and the cheese is melted.
6. Serve:
   - Remove the fried chile rellenos from the skillet and drain on paper towels to remove excess oil.
   - Serve hot with red salsa or enchilada sauce drizzled over the top.
   - Garnish with fresh cilantro leaves, if desired.

Enjoy your flavorful chile rellenos!

**Chimichurri Steak**

Ingredients

- 6 large poblano peppers
- 1 cup of shredded Monterey Jack cheese
- 1 cup of shredded cheddar cheese
- 1 cup of corn kernels (fresh or frozen)
- 1/2 cup of diced onion
- 2 cloves of garlic, minced
- 1/2 cup of all-purpose flour
- 4 large eggs, separated
- 1 teaspoon of salt
- Vegetable oil for frying
- Red salsa or enchilada sauce for serving
- Fresh cilantro leaves for garnish (optional)

Instructions

1. Roast and Peel the Peppers:
   - Preheat the broiler in your oven.
   - Place the poblano peppers on a baking sheet and broil, turning occasionally, until the skins are charred and blistered all over, about 8-10 minutes.
   - Transfer the roasted peppers to a bowl and cover with plastic wrap. Let them steam for about 10 minutes.
   - Once cooled, peel off the charred skins, then carefully make a slit lengthwise down one side of each pepper and remove the seeds and membranes.
2. Prepare the Filling:
   - In a skillet, heat a tablespoon of vegetable oil over medium heat.
   - Add the diced onion and minced garlic, cooking until softened, about 3 minutes.
   - Add the corn kernels and cook for another 2-3 minutes.
   - Remove from heat and let the mixture cool slightly.
   - In a bowl, mix together the shredded Monterey Jack cheese and shredded cheddar cheese. Add the cooled corn mixture and mix until well combined.
3. Fill the Peppers:
   - Stuff each roasted poblano pepper with the cheese and corn mixture, ensuring they are evenly filled.

4. Prepare the Batter:
   - In a large bowl, beat the egg whites with an electric mixer until stiff peaks form.
   - In a separate bowl, whisk the egg yolks with the flour and salt until smooth.
   - Gently fold the egg yolk mixture into the beaten egg whites until just combined.
5. Fry the Stuffed Peppers:
   - In a large skillet, heat about 1 inch of vegetable oil over medium-high heat until hot but not smoking.
   - Dip each stuffed poblano pepper into the egg batter, coating it evenly.
   - Carefully place the battered peppers in the hot oil, working in batches if necessary.
   - Fry the peppers for about 3-4 minutes on each side, or until they are golden brown and the cheese is melted.
6. Serve:
   - Remove the fried chile rellenos from the skillet and drain on paper towels to remove excess oil.
   - Serve hot with red salsa or enchilada sauce drizzled over the top.
   - Garnish with fresh cilantro leaves, if desired.

Enjoy your flavorful chile rellenos!

## Chimichurri Steak

Ingredients

- 4 steaks of your choice (such as ribeye, sirloin, or flank steak)
- Salt and pepper to taste

For the Chimichurri Sauce:

- 1 cup of fresh parsley, finely chopped
- 1/4 cup of fresh cilantro, finely chopped
- 4 cloves of garlic, minced
- 1/4 cup of red wine vinegar
- 1/2 cup of extra virgin olive oil
- 1 tablespoon of dried oregano
- 1 teaspoon of red pepper flakes (adjust to taste)
- Salt and pepper to taste
- Optional: 1 tablespoon of fresh lemon juice

Instructions

1. Prepare the Chimichurri Sauce:
    - In a medium bowl, combine the chopped parsley, chopped cilantro, minced garlic, red wine vinegar, olive oil, dried oregano, and red pepper flakes.
    - Season with salt and pepper to taste.
    - Optionally, add fresh lemon juice for an extra citrusy kick.
    - Mix well to combine. Taste and adjust seasoning if needed. Set aside to let the flavors meld while you prepare the steaks.
2. Prepare the Steaks:
    - Preheat your grill or grill pan to medium-high heat.
    - Season the steaks generously with salt and pepper on both sides.
3. Grill the Steaks:
    - Place the seasoned steaks on the preheated grill or grill pan.
    - Cook the steaks to your desired level of doneness, flipping them once halfway through the cooking time.
    - For medium-rare, grill for about 4-5 minutes per side, depending on the thickness of the steaks.
4. Rest the Steaks:
    - Once cooked to your liking, transfer the steaks to a plate and let them rest for a few minutes. This allows the juices to redistribute throughout the meat.

5. Serve:
    - Slice the rested steaks against the grain into thin strips.
    - Drizzle the chimichurri sauce generously over the sliced steaks or serve it on the side for dipping.
    - Optionally, garnish with additional fresh herbs or a sprinkle of red pepper flakes for extra flavor and visual appeal.

Enjoy your juicy and flavorful chimichurri steak!

**Churrasco**

Ingredients

- 2 lbs (900 g) of skirt steak or flank steak
- Salt and pepper to taste

For the Marinade:

- 1/4 cup of soy sauce
- 1/4 cup of olive oil
- 4 cloves of garlic, minced
- 2 tablespoons of fresh lime juice
- 1 tablespoon of Worcestershire sauce
- 1 teaspoon of ground cumin
- 1 teaspoon of paprika
- 1/2 teaspoon of red pepper flakes (optional)
- 2 tablespoons of chopped fresh cilantro or parsley

Instructions

1. Prepare the Marinade:
    - In a bowl, whisk together the soy sauce, olive oil, minced garlic, lime juice, Worcestershire sauce, ground cumin, paprika, red pepper flakes (if using), and chopped fresh cilantro or parsley.
2. Marinate the Steak:
    - Place the skirt steak or flank steak in a shallow dish or a resealable plastic bag.
    - Pour the marinade over the steak, making sure it is evenly coated.
    - Cover the dish or seal the bag, and refrigerate for at least 1 hour, or overnight for best results. Allow the steak to marinate in the refrigerator.
3. Preheat the Grill:
    - Preheat your grill to medium-high heat. If using a charcoal grill, wait until the coals are covered with white ash and are medium-hot.
4. Grill the Steak:
    - Remove the marinated steak from the refrigerator and let it come to room temperature for about 20-30 minutes.
    - Remove the steak from the marinade, shaking off any excess.
    - Season the steak generously with salt and pepper on both sides.

- Place the steak on the preheated grill and cook for about 4-5 minutes per side for medium-rare, or until desired doneness is reached. Cooking time may vary depending on the thickness of the steak and the heat of the grill.
- For cross-hatch grill marks, rotate the steak 45 degrees halfway through grilling on each side.

5. Rest the Steak:
    - Once cooked to your liking, transfer the steak to a cutting board and let it rest for 5-10 minutes. This allows the juices to redistribute throughout the meat.
6. Slice and Serve:
    - After resting, slice the steak against the grain into thin strips.
    - Serve the churrasco steak hot, with your choice of sides such as chimichurri sauce, grilled vegetables, rice, or salad.

Enjoy your delicious and flavorful churrasco steak!

# Cochinita Pibil

Ingredients

- 2 lbs (900 g) of pork shoulder, cut into 2-inch cubes
- 4 tablespoons of annatto (achiote) paste
- 1/2 cup of orange juice
- 1/4 cup of lime juice
- 4 cloves of garlic, minced
- 1 teaspoon of ground cumin
- 1 teaspoon of dried oregano
- 1 teaspoon of ground black pepper
- 1 teaspoon of salt
- 2 bay leaves
- 1/4 cup of white vinegar
- Banana leaves (optional, for wrapping)
- Corn tortillas, for serving
- Pickled red onions, for serving (optional)

Instructions

1. Marinate the Pork:
    - In a large bowl, combine the annatto paste, orange juice, lime juice, minced garlic, ground cumin, dried oregano, ground black pepper, salt, and white vinegar. Mix until the annatto paste is fully dissolved.
    - Add the cubed pork shoulder to the marinade, making sure each piece is well coated.
    - Cover the bowl with plastic wrap and refrigerate for at least 4 hours, or preferably overnight, to allow the flavors to meld.
2. Preheat the Oven:
    - Preheat your oven to 325°F (160°C).
3. Prepare the Banana Leaves (if using):
    - If using banana leaves to wrap the cochinita pibil, briefly pass them over an open flame to soften them. This will make them more pliable and prevent them from tearing.
4. Assemble and Cook:
    - Transfer the marinated pork and marinade to a baking dish or a Dutch oven.
    - Add the bay leaves to the dish.

- If using banana leaves, line the baking dish with them and fold them over the pork to cover completely. Otherwise, cover the dish tightly with aluminum foil.
- Place the dish in the preheated oven and bake for about 3-4 hours, or until the pork is tender and easily shreds with a fork.

5. Serve:
    - Once cooked, remove the cochinita pibil from the oven.
    - Serve the cochinita pibil hot, accompanied by warm corn tortillas for making tacos.
    - Optionally, serve with pickled red onions on the side for added flavor.

Enjoy your authentic and flavorful Cochinita Pibil!

**Empanadas**

Dough Ingredients:

- 3 cups of all-purpose flour
- 1 teaspoon of salt
- 1/2 cup of unsalted butter, cold and cut into small cubes
- 1 large egg
- 1/2 cup of cold water
- 1 tablespoon of white vinegar or lemon juice

Filling Ingredients:

- 1 tablespoon of vegetable oil
- 1 small onion, finely chopped
- 2 cloves of garlic, minced
- 1 lb (450 g) of ground beef or chicken
- 1 teaspoon of ground cumin
- 1 teaspoon of paprika
- 1/2 teaspoon of dried oregano
- Salt and pepper to taste
- 1/2 cup of green olives, chopped (optional)
- 1/2 cup of raisins (optional)
- 2 hard-boiled eggs, chopped (optional)

Assembly and Cooking:

- 1 egg, beaten (for egg wash)
- Vegetable oil, for frying or baking

Instructions:

1. Prepare the Dough:
    - In a large bowl, combine the flour and salt.
    - Add the cold, cubed butter to the flour mixture.
    - Using a pastry cutter or your fingertips, work the butter into the flour until the mixture resembles coarse crumbs.
    - In a separate small bowl, beat the egg with the cold water and vinegar or lemon juice.
    - Gradually add the egg mixture to the flour mixture, stirring until the dough comes together.

- Turn the dough out onto a floured surface and knead gently until smooth.
- Wrap the dough in plastic wrap and refrigerate for at least 30 minutes.

2. Prepare the Filling:
   - In a skillet, heat the vegetable oil over medium heat.
   - Add the chopped onion and garlic, cooking until softened.
   - Add the ground beef or chicken to the skillet, breaking it up with a spoon.
   - Cook until the meat is browned and cooked through.
   - Stir in the ground cumin, paprika, dried oregano, salt, and pepper.
   - If using, add the chopped green olives, raisins, and hard-boiled eggs. Mix well.
   - Remove the skillet from the heat and let the filling cool to room temperature.

3. Assemble the Empanadas:
   - Preheat your oven to 375°F (190°C) if baking, or heat vegetable oil in a deep fryer or skillet if frying.
   - On a floured surface, roll out the chilled dough to about 1/8 inch thickness.
   - Using a round cutter or a small plate, cut out circles of dough.
   - Place a spoonful of the filling in the center of each dough circle.
   - Fold the dough over the filling to form a half-moon shape.
   - Press the edges together firmly to seal, then crimp with a fork to create a decorative edge.

4. Cook the Empanadas:
   - If baking, place the assembled empanadas on a baking sheet lined with parchment paper.
   - Brush the tops of the empanadas with beaten egg for a golden finish.
   - Bake in the preheated oven for 20-25 minutes, or until golden brown.
   - If frying, carefully lower the empanadas into the hot oil and fry until golden brown on both sides, about 3-4 minutes per side.
   - Remove the fried empanadas from the oil and drain on paper towels.

5. Serve:
   - Serve the empanadas hot, with your favorite dipping sauce or salsa on the side.

Enjoy your delicious homemade empanadas!

# Enchiladas

Ingredients:

For the Enchilada Sauce:

- 2 tablespoons of vegetable oil
- 2 tablespoons of all-purpose flour
- 4 tablespoons of chili powder
- 1/2 teaspoon of ground cumin
- 1/4 teaspoon of dried oregano
- 1/4 teaspoon of garlic powder
- 2 cups of chicken or vegetable broth
- Salt and pepper to taste

For the Filling:

- 2 cups of cooked and shredded chicken or beef
- 1 small onion, finely chopped
- 1 clove of garlic, minced
- 1 can (4 oz) of diced green chilies, drained
- 1/2 cup of corn kernels (fresh, frozen, or canned)
- 1/2 cup of black beans, drained and rinsed (optional)
- 1 cup of shredded cheese (cheddar, Monterey Jack, or a blend)
- Salt and pepper to taste

For Assembly:

- 12 corn tortillas
- Vegetable oil, for softening the tortillas
- Additional shredded cheese for topping
- Chopped fresh cilantro, for garnish
- Sour cream, for serving (optional)
- Sliced jalapeños, for serving (optional)

Instructions:

1. Prepare the Enchilada Sauce:
    - In a saucepan, heat the vegetable oil over medium heat.
    - Add the flour and whisk constantly for 1-2 minutes to form a roux.
    - Stir in the chili powder, ground cumin, dried oregano, and garlic powder. Cook for another minute.

- Gradually whisk in the chicken or vegetable broth until the sauce is smooth.
- Bring the sauce to a simmer and cook for 5-7 minutes, or until it thickens slightly.
- Season with salt and pepper to taste. Set aside.

2. **Prepare the Filling:**
   - In a skillet, heat a tablespoon of vegetable oil over medium heat.
   - Add the chopped onion and minced garlic, cooking until softened.
   - Add the shredded chicken or beef, diced green chilies, corn kernels, and black beans (if using). Cook for 2-3 minutes until heated through.
   - Season with salt and pepper to taste. Remove from heat and set aside.

3. **Assemble the Enchiladas:**
   - Preheat your oven to 350°F (175°C).
   - Soften the corn tortillas by heating them briefly in a skillet with a little vegetable oil, flipping once, until they are pliable.
   - Spoon a portion of the filling mixture onto each tortilla and roll it up tightly.
   - Place the rolled enchiladas seam-side down in a baking dish.

4. **Top with Sauce and Cheese:**
   - Pour the enchilada sauce evenly over the top of the rolled enchiladas.
   - Sprinkle shredded cheese over the top.

5. **Bake:**
   - Cover the baking dish with aluminum foil and bake in the preheated oven for 20-25 minutes, or until the cheese is melted and bubbly.

6. **Serve:**
   - Remove the enchiladas from the oven and let them cool slightly.
   - Garnish with chopped fresh cilantro.
   - Serve hot, with sour cream and sliced jalapeños on the side if desired.

Enjoy your delicious homemade enchiladas!

**Feijoada**

Ingredients:

- 1 lb (450 g) of black beans, dried
- 1 lb (450 g) of pork shoulder, cubed
- 1 lb (450 g) of smoked sausage or linguica, sliced
- 1 lb (450 g) of pork ribs or bacon
- 1 lb (450 g) of beef ribs or brisket
- 1 large onion, chopped
- 4 cloves of garlic, minced
- 2 bay leaves
- 1 tablespoon of olive oil
- Salt and black pepper to taste
- Water, as needed

Optional Side Dishes:

- White rice
- Farofa (toasted cassava flour)
- Orange slices
- Collard greens, sautéed
- Hot sauce

Instructions:

1. Prepare the Beans:
    - Rinse the black beans under cold water and remove any debris.
    - Place the beans in a large pot and cover with water. Let them soak overnight or for at least 8 hours.
2. Cook the Meats:
    - In a large skillet, heat the olive oil over medium heat.
    - Add the cubed pork shoulder, sliced sausage, pork ribs or bacon, and beef ribs or brisket. Cook until browned on all sides.
    - Transfer the cooked meats to a large Dutch oven or stockpot.
3. Prepare the Feijoada:
    - Drain the soaked black beans and add them to the pot with the cooked meats.
    - Add the chopped onion, minced garlic, and bay leaves to the pot.
    - Season with salt and black pepper to taste.
    - Add enough water to cover all the ingredients in the pot.

4. Simmer the Feijoada:
    - Bring the pot to a boil over high heat, then reduce the heat to low.
    - Cover and simmer for 2-3 hours, or until the beans are tender and the meats are cooked through and tender. Stir occasionally and add more water if necessary to keep the beans covered.
5. Serve:
    - Once the feijoada is ready, remove the bay leaves and discard.
    - Serve the feijoada hot with white rice, farofa, orange slices, sautéed collard greens, and hot sauce on the side.
    - Enjoy your traditional Brazilian feast!

Feijoada is often enjoyed as a communal meal, so invite friends and family to join you for a delicious and hearty dining experience.

**Flautas**

Ingredients:

- 12 corn tortillas
- 2 cups of cooked and shredded chicken or beef
- 1 cup of shredded cheese (cheddar, Monterey Jack, or a blend)
- 1/2 cup of diced onion
- 1/2 cup of diced green chilies (canned or fresh)
- 2 cloves of garlic, minced
- 1 teaspoon of ground cumin
- 1 teaspoon of chili powder
- Salt and pepper to taste
- Vegetable oil, for frying
- Optional toppings: shredded lettuce, diced tomatoes, sour cream, guacamole, salsa

Instructions:

1. Prepare the Filling:
    - In a skillet, heat a tablespoon of vegetable oil over medium heat.
    - Add the diced onion and minced garlic, cooking until softened.
    - Add the shredded chicken or beef to the skillet, along with the diced green chilies, ground cumin, chili powder, salt, and pepper. Cook for 2-3 minutes until heated through and well combined.
    - Remove the skillet from the heat and let the filling cool slightly.
2. Assemble the Flautas:
    - Place a small amount of the filling mixture in the center of each corn tortilla.
    - Sprinkle a little shredded cheese over the filling.
    - Roll up each tortilla tightly around the filling to form a flute-like shape.
    - Secure the flautas with toothpicks to hold them together.
3. Fry the Flautas:
    - In a large skillet, heat about 1 inch of vegetable oil over medium-high heat until hot but not smoking.
    - Carefully place the flautas in the hot oil, seam side down, and fry in batches until golden brown and crispy on all sides, about 2-3 minutes per side.
    - Use tongs to carefully turn the flautas to ensure even frying.

- Once cooked, transfer the flautas to a plate lined with paper towels to drain any excess oil.
4. Serve:
    - Serve the flautas hot, with your choice of toppings such as shredded lettuce, diced tomatoes, sour cream, guacamole, and salsa.
    - Optionally, remove the toothpicks before serving.

Enjoy your crispy and delicious flautas as a tasty appetizer, snack, or main dish!

**Gallo Pinto**

Ingredients:

- 2 cups of cooked white rice
- 1 cup of cooked black beans (or red beans), drained and rinsed
- 1 small onion, finely chopped
- 1 bell pepper (red or green), finely chopped
- 2 cloves of garlic, minced
- 2 tablespoons of vegetable oil
- 1/2 teaspoon of ground cumin
- 1/2 teaspoon of paprika
- Salt and pepper to taste
- Optional: chopped cilantro for garnish
- Optional: hot sauce or salsa for serving

Instructions:

1. Prepare the Ingredients:
    - If you haven't already, cook the white rice according to package instructions until tender. Let it cool slightly before using.
    - Cook the black beans separately until tender, then drain and rinse them under cold water. Set aside.
2. Sauté the Aromatics:
    - In a large skillet or frying pan, heat the vegetable oil over medium heat.
    - Add the chopped onion and bell pepper to the skillet. Sauté until they start to soften, about 3-4 minutes.
    - Add the minced garlic and cook for another minute until fragrant.
3. Add the Beans and Spices:
    - Stir in the cooked black beans, ground cumin, and paprika. Mix well with the sautéed aromatics.
4. Add the Rice:
    - Add the cooked white rice to the skillet with the bean mixture.
    - Stir everything together until well combined.
5. Season and Cook:
    - Season the gallo pinto with salt and pepper to taste. Stir well to distribute the seasoning evenly.
    - Cook the mixture for an additional 5-7 minutes, stirring occasionally, until heated through and well combined.
6. Serve:

- Once the gallo pinto is ready, remove the skillet from the heat.
- Garnish with chopped cilantro if desired.
- Serve hot as a side dish or main course, accompanied by hot sauce or salsa for extra flavor.

Gallo pinto is a versatile and flavorful dish that can be enjoyed for breakfast, lunch, or dinner. It pairs well with fried eggs, avocado slices, and fried plantains for a traditional Costa Rican meal. Enjoy!

# Hallacas

Dough Ingredients:

- 4 cups of precooked corn flour (masa harina)
- 4 cups of warm water
- 1 cup of vegetable oil or melted butter
- 1 teaspoon of salt

Filling Ingredients:

- 2 lbs (900 g) of pork shoulder or beef, cooked and shredded
- 1/2 lb (225 g) of bacon, diced
- 1/2 lb (225 g) of smoked ham, diced
- 1/2 cup of raisins
- 1/2 cup of capers
- 1/2 cup of green olives, sliced
- 1/2 cup of chopped onion
- 1/2 cup of chopped bell pepper
- 1/4 cup of chopped cilantro
- 1/4 cup of chopped green onions
- 1/4 cup of chopped parsley
- 4 cloves of garlic, minced
- 2 teaspoons of ground cumin
- 2 teaspoons of paprika
- 1 teaspoon of ground black pepper
- Salt to taste
- 1/2 cup of vegetable oil
- 1/2 cup of beef or chicken broth

Banana Leaves and String for Wrapping

Instructions:

1. Prepare the Filling:
    - In a large skillet, heat the vegetable oil over medium heat.
    - Add the diced onion, chopped bell pepper, and minced garlic. Sauté until softened.
    - Add the shredded pork or beef, diced bacon, diced ham, raisins, capers, sliced green olives, chopped cilantro, chopped green onions, chopped

parsley, ground cumin, paprika, black pepper, and salt to taste. Cook until the flavors are well combined, about 10 minutes.
- Pour in the beef or chicken broth and simmer for another 5 minutes. Remove from heat and let the filling cool.

2. Prepare the Dough:
   - In a large mixing bowl, combine the precooked corn flour (masa harina) with warm water, vegetable oil or melted butter, and salt. Mix until a soft and smooth dough forms.

3. Assemble the Hallacas:
   - Rinse the banana leaves and cut them into squares, approximately 10x10 inches (25x25 cm).
   - Place a banana leaf square on a clean work surface.
   - Spread a thin layer of dough (about 1/4 inch thick) on the banana leaf square, leaving a border around the edges.
   - Spoon a portion of the filling onto the center of the dough.
   - Fold the sides of the banana leaf over the filling to form a rectangular packet. Fold the ends to seal the hallaca. Secure with string if necessary.
   - Repeat the process with the remaining dough and filling.

4. Cook the Hallacas:
   - Bring a large pot of water to a boil.
   - Carefully place the hallacas in the boiling water and cook for about 1 to 1.5 hours, or until the dough is cooked through and the filling is heated.
   - Remove the hallacas from the water and let them cool slightly before serving.

5. Serve:
   - Serve the hallacas warm, either as a main dish or as a festive holiday meal. They can be accompanied by salad, avocado, and/or hot sauce according to preference.

Hallacas are traditionally enjoyed during the Christmas season in Venezuela. They require some effort to prepare but are worth it for their delicious flavor and festive significance. Enjoy sharing this special dish with family and friends!

## Huevos Rancheros

Ingredients:

- 4 large eggs
- 4 corn tortillas
- 1 cup of cooked black beans (or refried beans)
- 1 cup of salsa (homemade or store-bought)
- 1/2 cup of shredded cheese (cheddar, Monterey Jack, or a blend)
- 1 avocado, sliced
- 1/4 cup of chopped fresh cilantro (optional)
- Salt and pepper to taste
- Olive oil or vegetable oil, for cooking

Instructions:

1. Cook the Eggs:
    - Heat a tablespoon of olive oil or vegetable oil in a skillet over medium heat.
    - Crack the eggs into the skillet, leaving space between them.
    - Season the eggs with salt and pepper to taste.
    - Cook the eggs until the whites are set but the yolks are still runny, about 3-4 minutes. You can cover the skillet with a lid for the last minute of cooking if you prefer firmer yolks.
2. Warm the Tortillas:
    - Heat the corn tortillas in a separate skillet or in the microwave until warm and pliable.
3. Assemble the Huevos Rancheros:
    - Place a warm tortilla on each plate.
    - Spread a layer of cooked black beans or refried beans over each tortilla.
    - Top the beans with a spoonful of salsa.
    - Carefully place a cooked egg on top of each tortilla.
4. Add Toppings:
    - Sprinkle shredded cheese over the eggs while they are still hot so that it melts slightly.
    - Garnish with sliced avocado and chopped fresh cilantro, if desired.
5. Serve:
    - Serve the huevos rancheros immediately, while they are still warm.
    - Optionally, serve with additional salsa on the side for extra flavor.

Huevos rancheros make a delicious and satisfying breakfast or brunch dish. Enjoy the combination of savory beans, spicy salsa, creamy avocado, and perfectly cooked eggs all served on a warm tortilla!

**Lomo Saltado**

Ingredients:

For the Marinade:

- 1 lb (450 g) of beef tenderloin or sirloin steak, thinly sliced
- 3 tablespoons of soy sauce
- 2 tablespoons of red wine vinegar
- 2 cloves of garlic, minced
- 1 teaspoon of ground cumin
- 1 teaspoon of paprika
- Salt and pepper to taste

For the Stir-fry:

- 2 tablespoons of vegetable oil
- 1 onion, thinly sliced
- 1 bell pepper, thinly sliced
- 2 tomatoes, sliced into wedges
- 1 jalapeño or chili pepper, thinly sliced (optional, for extra heat)
- 2 cloves of garlic, minced
- 1 tablespoon of soy sauce
- 1 tablespoon of red wine vinegar
- 1/4 cup of beef or chicken broth
- Fresh cilantro leaves, chopped, for garnish
- Cooked white rice, for serving

Instructions:

1. Marinate the Beef:
    - In a bowl, combine the thinly sliced beef with soy sauce, red wine vinegar, minced garlic, ground cumin, paprika, salt, and pepper.
    - Mix well to ensure the beef is evenly coated with the marinade.
    - Let the beef marinate for at least 30 minutes, or preferably for a few hours, in the refrigerator.
2. Stir-fry the Beef:
    - Heat 1 tablespoon of vegetable oil in a large skillet or wok over high heat.
    - Once the oil is hot, add the marinated beef in batches, spreading it out in a single layer to ensure it cooks evenly.

- Stir-fry the beef for 2-3 minutes, or until it is browned and cooked through. Remove the beef from the skillet and set aside.
3. Cook the Vegetables:
    - In the same skillet or wok, add another tablespoon of vegetable oil.
    - Add the sliced onion, bell pepper, tomatoes, and jalapeño or chili pepper (if using) to the skillet.
    - Stir-fry the vegetables for 3-4 minutes, or until they are tender-crisp.
    - Add the minced garlic to the skillet and cook for an additional minute, stirring constantly.
4. Combine and Season:
    - Return the cooked beef to the skillet with the vegetables.
    - Pour in the soy sauce, red wine vinegar, and beef or chicken broth.
    - Stir everything together and cook for another 1-2 minutes, allowing the flavors to meld and the sauce to slightly thicken.
    - Taste and adjust the seasoning with salt and pepper if needed.
5. Serve:
    - Garnish the lomo saltado with chopped fresh cilantro leaves.
    - Serve hot over cooked white rice.

Enjoy your flavorful and aromatic lomo saltado, a classic Peruvian stir-fry dish that combines tender beef, colorful vegetables, and bold spices!

**Mofongo**

Ingredients:

- 4 green plantains
- 4 cloves of garlic, minced
- 4 tablespoons of olive oil or lard
- Salt to taste
- Optional: crispy pork rinds (chicharrones) for garnish

Instructions:

1. Prepare the Plantains:
    - Peel the green plantains and cut them into 1-inch-thick slices.
2. Fry the Plantains:
    - Heat the olive oil or lard in a large skillet over medium heat.
    - Fry the plantain slices in the hot oil until golden brown and cooked through, about 5 minutes per side.
    - Remove the fried plantain slices from the skillet and drain them on paper towels to remove excess oil.
3. Make the Mofongo:
    - In a large mortar and pestle or a sturdy bowl, add the fried plantain slices and minced garlic.
    - Use the pestle or a potato masher to mash the plantains and garlic together until they form a coarse mixture.
    - Gradually add the olive oil or lard, a tablespoon at a time, while continuing to mash, until the mofongo reaches your desired consistency. It should be smooth and moldable, but not too wet.
    - Season the mofongo with salt to taste and mix well to incorporate.
4. Shape and Serve:
    - To shape the mofongo, you can use a small bowl or a mofongo mold if available. Press the mofongo mixture firmly into the mold or bowl to compact it.
    - Carefully unmold the shaped mofongo onto a serving plate.
    - Garnish with crispy pork rinds (chicharrones) if desired.
    - Serve the mofongo hot as a side dish or as a main course, accompanied by your favorite protein and sauce.

Enjoy the delicious flavors and textures of this traditional Puerto Rican dish! Mofongo is a versatile dish that pairs well with a variety of meats, seafood, and sauces.

**Moqueca**

Ingredients:

For the Fish Marinade:

- 1 lb (450 g) of firm white fish fillets (such as cod, tilapia, or snapper), cut into chunks
- 2 cloves of garlic, minced
- 2 tablespoons of lime juice
- Salt and pepper to taste

For the Moqueca:

- 2 tablespoons of olive oil
- 1 onion, thinly sliced
- 1 bell pepper (red or green), thinly sliced
- 2 tomatoes, chopped
- 3 cloves of garlic, minced
- 1 tablespoon of tomato paste
- 1 tablespoon of paprika
- 1/2 teaspoon of ground cumin
- 1/2 teaspoon of ground coriander
- 1/2 teaspoon of red pepper flakes (adjust to taste)
- 1 cup of coconut milk
- 1/2 cup of fish or vegetable broth
- Salt and pepper to taste
- Chopped fresh cilantro or parsley for garnish
- Cooked white rice, for serving

Instructions:

1. Marinate the Fish:
    - In a bowl, combine the fish chunks with minced garlic, lime juice, salt, and pepper.
    - Let the fish marinate for at least 15-20 minutes while you prepare the rest of the dish.
2. Prepare the Moqueca:
    - In a large skillet or Dutch oven, heat the olive oil over medium heat.
    - Add the thinly sliced onion and bell pepper to the skillet. Sauté until softened, about 5 minutes.

- Add the chopped tomatoes and minced garlic to the skillet. Cook for another 2-3 minutes until the tomatoes begin to soften.
    - Stir in the tomato paste, paprika, ground cumin, ground coriander, and red pepper flakes. Cook for 1-2 minutes until fragrant.
    - Pour in the coconut milk and fish or vegetable broth. Bring the mixture to a simmer.
3. Add the Fish:
    - Carefully add the marinated fish chunks to the simmering liquid in the skillet.
    - Gently stir to combine, making sure the fish is submerged in the liquid.
    - Cover the skillet and let the fish cook in the simmering liquid for about 8-10 minutes, or until cooked through and flaky.
4. Season and Serve:
    - Taste the moqueca and season with salt and pepper to taste.
    - Garnish with chopped fresh cilantro or parsley.
    - Serve hot over cooked white rice.

Enjoy the rich and flavorful taste of Brazilian moqueca de peixe, a delightful fish stew with a tropical twist!

**Pabellón Criollo**

Ingredients:

For the Shredded Beef:

- 1 lb (450 g) of flank steak or skirt steak
- 1 onion, quartered
- 4 cloves of garlic, smashed
- 1 bay leaf
- Salt and pepper to taste
- Water

For the Black Beans:

- 1 cup of black beans, dried
- 1 onion, chopped
- 2 cloves of garlic, minced
- 1 bell pepper, chopped
- 1 tablespoon of vegetable oil
- 1 teaspoon of ground cumin
- Salt and pepper to taste

For the Rice:

- 1 cup of white rice
- 2 cups of water
- Salt to taste

For the Plantains:

- 2 ripe plantains, sliced
- Vegetable oil for frying

For Serving:

- Shredded white cheese (queso blanco or queso fresco)
- Avocado slices
- Optional: arepas or cornbread

Instructions:

1. Cook the Shredded Beef:

- Place the flank steak or skirt steak in a large pot. Add the quartered onion, smashed garlic cloves, bay leaf, salt, and pepper.
- Cover the meat with water and bring to a boil over medium-high heat.
- Reduce the heat to low and simmer, partially covered, for about 2-3 hours, or until the meat is tender and easily shreds with a fork.
- Once cooked, remove the meat from the pot and shred it using two forks. Set aside.

2. Prepare the Black Beans:
    - Rinse the black beans under cold water and remove any debris.
    - In a large pot, heat the vegetable oil over medium heat. Add the chopped onion, minced garlic, and bell pepper. Sauté until softened.
    - Add the black beans to the pot along with enough water to cover them by about 2 inches.
    - Stir in the ground cumin, salt, and pepper.
    - Bring the beans to a boil, then reduce the heat to low and simmer, partially covered, for about 1.5 to 2 hours, or until the beans are tender. Add more water if needed during cooking.
    - Once the beans are cooked, mash some of them against the side of the pot with a spoon to thicken the broth slightly.

3. Cook the Rice:
    - Rinse the rice under cold water until the water runs clear.
    - In a saucepan, combine the rice, water, and salt. Bring to a boil over high heat.
    - Reduce the heat to low, cover the saucepan, and simmer for 18-20 minutes, or until the rice is cooked and the water is absorbed. Fluff the rice with a fork.

4. Fry the Plantains:
    - Heat vegetable oil in a skillet over medium heat.
    - Fry the plantain slices until golden brown on both sides, about 2-3 minutes per side. Remove from the skillet and drain on paper towels.

5. Assemble the Pabellón Criollo:
    - To serve, place a portion of cooked rice on a plate.
    - Top the rice with a generous serving of shredded beef and black beans.
    - Arrange the fried plantain slices on the side.
    - Garnish with shredded white cheese and avocado slices.
    - Optionally, serve with arepas or cornbread on the side.

Enjoy the delicious and comforting flavors of Pabellón Criollo, a traditional Venezuelan dish that combines tender shredded beef, savory black beans, sweet fried plantains, and fluffy rice!

## Pastel de Choclo

Ingredients:

For the Corn Filling:

- 6 ears of corn on the cob, kernels removed (about 6 cups of corn kernels)
- 1 onion, chopped
- 2 cloves of garlic, minced
- 1 red bell pepper, chopped
- 1 tablespoon of vegetable oil
- 1 teaspoon of ground cumin
- 1 teaspoon of paprika
- Salt and pepper to taste
- 1/2 cup of milk
- 1/4 cup of fresh basil leaves, chopped

For the Beef Filling:

- 1 lb (450 g) of ground beef
- 1 onion, chopped
- 2 cloves of garlic, minced
- 1 teaspoon of ground cumin
- 1 teaspoon of paprika
- Salt and pepper to taste
- 1/2 cup of pitted black olives, sliced
- 2 hard-boiled eggs, sliced

For the Corn Batter:

- 4 cups of corn kernels (from about 6-8 ears of corn)
- 1/2 cup of milk
- 2 tablespoons of granulated sugar
- Salt to taste

For Assembly:

- 1 tablespoon of butter, melted
- 1/2 cup of grated Parmesan cheese

Instructions:

1. Prepare the Corn Filling:
   - In a skillet, heat the vegetable oil over medium heat.
   - Add the chopped onion and minced garlic, and sauté until softened.
   - Add the red bell pepper and continue to cook for another 2-3 minutes.
   - Stir in the ground cumin, paprika, salt, and pepper.
   - Add the corn kernels and cook for about 5-7 minutes, or until the corn is tender.
   - Pour in the milk and simmer for another 2-3 minutes.
   - Stir in the chopped basil leaves and remove from heat. Set aside.
2. Prepare the Beef Filling:
   - In a separate skillet, cook the ground beef over medium heat until browned and cooked through.
   - Add the chopped onion and minced garlic to the skillet with the beef, and sauté until softened.
   - Stir in the ground cumin, paprika, salt, and pepper.
   - Add the sliced black olives and cook for another 2-3 minutes.
   - Remove from heat and set aside.
3. Prepare the Corn Batter:
   - In a blender or food processor, blend the corn kernels with milk, sugar, and salt until smooth.
4. Assemble the Pastel de Choclo:
   - Preheat your oven to 375°F (190°C).
   - Grease a large baking dish with butter.
   - Spread half of the corn batter in the bottom of the baking dish.
   - Next, layer the beef filling evenly over the corn batter.
   - Arrange the sliced hard-boiled eggs over the beef filling.
   - Spread the corn filling over the eggs.
   - Pour the remaining corn batter over the top, spreading it evenly to cover the filling.
   - Sprinkle the grated Parmesan cheese over the top.
   - Bake in the preheated oven for 35-40 minutes, or until the top is golden brown and set.
5. Serve:
   - Allow the Pastel de Choclo to cool for a few minutes before serving.
   - Cut into squares and serve warm.

Enjoy this delicious and comforting Chilean dish with family and friends!

**Pastelitos**

Ingredients:

For the Dough:

- 2 cups of all-purpose flour
- 1 teaspoon of salt
- 1/2 cup of unsalted butter, cold and cubed
- 1/2 cup of cold water

For the Filling:

- 1 lb (450 g) of ground beef or ground chicken
- 1 onion, finely chopped
- 2 cloves of garlic, minced
- 1 bell pepper, finely chopped
- 1 tomato, finely chopped
- 1 teaspoon of ground cumin
- 1 teaspoon of paprika
- Salt and pepper to taste
- Vegetable oil for frying

Instructions:

1. Prepare the Dough:
    - In a large mixing bowl, combine the all-purpose flour and salt.
    - Add the cold, cubed butter to the flour mixture.
    - Using a pastry cutter or your fingers, work the butter into the flour until the mixture resembles coarse crumbs.
    - Gradually add the cold water, a little at a time, and mix until the dough comes together.
    - Transfer the dough to a lightly floured surface and knead it gently until smooth.
    - Wrap the dough in plastic wrap and refrigerate for at least 30 minutes.
2. Prepare the Filling:
    - In a skillet, heat a tablespoon of vegetable oil over medium heat.
    - Add the chopped onion and bell pepper to the skillet. Sauté until softened.
    - Add the minced garlic and cook for another minute until fragrant.
    - Add the ground beef or chicken to the skillet. Cook until browned, breaking it apart with a spoon as it cooks.

- Stir in the chopped tomato, ground cumin, paprika, salt, and pepper. Cook for another 5-7 minutes, or until the mixture is well combined and any excess liquid has evaporated.
- Remove the skillet from the heat and let the filling cool completely.

3. Assemble the Pastelitos:
    - Preheat your oven to 375°F (190°C).
    - On a lightly floured surface, roll out the chilled dough to about 1/8 inch thickness.
    - Use a round cutter or a glass to cut out circles from the dough.
    - Place a spoonful of the cooled filling in the center of each dough circle.
    - Fold the dough over the filling to create a half-moon shape. Use a fork to crimp the edges and seal the pastelitos.
    - Place the assembled pastelitos on a baking sheet lined with parchment paper.

4. Bake the Pastelitos:
    - Brush the tops of the pastelitos with a little beaten egg or milk for a golden finish (optional).
    - Bake in the preheated oven for 20-25 minutes, or until the pastelitos are golden brown and crispy.

5. Serve:
    - Remove the pastelitos from the oven and let them cool for a few minutes before serving.
    - Enjoy the pastelitos warm as a delicious snack or appetizer.

These pastelitos are perfect for serving at parties or enjoying as a tasty snack any time of day!

**Patacones**

Ingredients:

- 2 green (unripe) plantains
- Vegetable oil for frying
- Salt to taste

Instructions:

1. Prepare the Plantains:
    - Start by peeling the green plantains. To peel them, cut off the ends of the plantains, then make shallow cuts along the length of the plantain. Carefully remove the peel by sliding your thumb under the skin and lifting it away.
    - Cut the peeled plantains into thick slices, about 1 inch (2.5 cm) thick.
2. Fry the Plantains:
    - In a large skillet or frying pan, heat enough vegetable oil over medium-high heat to cover the bottom of the pan and have a depth of about 1/2 inch (1.25 cm).
    - Once the oil is hot, carefully add the plantain slices to the pan in a single layer, making sure not to overcrowd the pan. You may need to fry them in batches.
    - Fry the plantain slices for about 2-3 minutes on each side, or until they are golden brown and cooked through.
    - Use a slotted spoon or tongs to transfer the fried plantain slices to a paper towel-lined plate to drain any excess oil.
3. Flatten the Plantains:
    - Once all the plantain slices are fried, place them on a cutting board or flat surface.
    - Use the bottom of a glass or a flat utensil to gently flatten each plantain slice into a disk. Press down firmly but be careful not to break them apart.
4. Fry Again:
    - Return the flattened plantains to the hot oil in the skillet.
    - Fry them for an additional 1-2 minutes on each side, or until they are crispy and golden brown.
    - Again, transfer the fried plantains to a paper towel-lined plate to drain any excess oil.
5. Season and Serve:

- Sprinkle the hot patacones with salt to taste immediately after frying while they are still warm.
- Serve the patacones as a delicious appetizer or side dish alongside your favorite dipping sauce, such as guacamole, salsa, or chimichurri.

Enjoy the crispy and savory goodness of homemade patacones! They are a popular and delicious snack in many Latin American countries.

## Pernil

Ingredients:

- 1 (5-7 pound) pork shoulder (also known as pork butt or picnic shoulder), bone-in
- 8 cloves of garlic, minced
- 2 tablespoons of olive oil
- 2 tablespoons of orange juice
- 2 tablespoons of white vinegar
- 2 tablespoons of dried oregano
- 1 tablespoon of ground cumin
- 1 tablespoon of paprika
- 1 tablespoon of salt
- 1 teaspoon of black pepper
- 1 teaspoon of dried thyme
- 1 teaspoon of dried rosemary
- 1 teaspoon of dried basil
- 1 teaspoon of dried parsley
- 1 teaspoon of adobo seasoning (optional)
- 1/2 cup of fresh orange juice (for basting)

Instructions:

1. Prepare the Marinade:
   - In a small bowl, combine the minced garlic, olive oil, orange juice, white vinegar, dried oregano, ground cumin, paprika, salt, black pepper, dried thyme, dried rosemary, dried basil, dried parsley, and adobo seasoning (if using). Mix well to form a paste.
2. Marinate the Pork:
   - Place the pork shoulder in a large roasting pan or a large resealable plastic bag.
   - Rub the marinade all over the pork, making sure to coat it evenly.
   - Cover the pork with plastic wrap (if using a roasting pan) or seal the bag, and refrigerate for at least 4 hours, or preferably overnight, to allow the flavors to meld.
3. Preheat the Oven:
   - Remove the marinated pork from the refrigerator and let it sit at room temperature for about 30 minutes before cooking.
   - Preheat your oven to 325°F (165°C).
4. Roast the Pork:

- Place the marinated pork shoulder in the preheated oven, uncovered.
- Roast the pork for about 20 minutes per pound, or until the internal temperature reaches 190-200°F (88-93°C) and the meat is tender and easily shreds with a fork.
- Baste the pork occasionally with fresh orange juice while it cooks to keep it moist and flavorful.

5. Rest and Serve:
   - Once the pork is fully cooked, remove it from the oven and tent it loosely with aluminum foil.
   - Let the pork rest for about 20-30 minutes before slicing and serving.
   - Serve the pernil slices with your favorite sides, such as rice and beans, plantains, or salad.

Enjoy the delicious flavors of this Puerto Rican-style roast pork, known for its tender and succulent meat with a flavorful crust!

**Picadillo**

Ingredients:

- 1 tablespoon olive oil
- 1 onion, finely chopped
- 2 cloves garlic, minced
- 1 bell pepper, diced
- 1 lb (450 g) ground beef or ground turkey
- 2 tomatoes, diced
- 1/4 cup tomato sauce
- 1/4 cup green olives, sliced
- 2 tablespoons capers
- 1/4 cup raisins
- 1 teaspoon ground cumin
- 1 teaspoon paprika
- Salt and pepper to taste
- Cooked white rice, for serving
- Fresh cilantro or parsley, chopped, for garnish (optional)

Instructions:

1. Sauté Aromatics:
    - Heat olive oil in a large skillet over medium heat. Add chopped onion, minced garlic, and diced bell pepper. Sauté until softened, about 3-4 minutes.
2. Brown the Meat:
    - Add ground beef or turkey to the skillet. Break it apart with a spatula and cook until browned, about 5-6 minutes.
3. Add Tomatoes and Sauce:
    - Stir in diced tomatoes and tomato sauce. Cook for another 2-3 minutes until the tomatoes soften and release their juices.
4. Incorporate Flavorings:
    - Add sliced green olives, capers, and raisins to the skillet. Sprinkle ground cumin and paprika over the mixture. Stir well to combine.
5. Simmer and Season:
    - Reduce heat to low and let the picadillo simmer for 10-15 minutes, allowing the flavors to meld together.
    - Season with salt and pepper to taste.
6. Serve:

- Serve the picadillo hot over cooked white rice.
- Garnish with chopped fresh cilantro or parsley if desired.

Enjoy the savory and flavorful goodness of this classic Latin American dish! Picadillo is versatile and can be enjoyed on its own, with rice, or as a filling for tacos, empanadas, or stuffed peppers.

## Picanha

Ingredients:

- 1 whole picanha (approximately 3-4 pounds)
- Coarse salt (preferably rock salt or sea salt)
- Optional: garlic powder, black pepper, or other seasonings of your choice

Instructions:

1. Prepare the Picanha:
    - Picanha is a cut of beef that comes from the top sirloin cap. It typically has a thick layer of fat on one side. Begin by trimming any excess fat on the surface of the picanha, leaving a thin layer to help baste the meat as it cooks.
2. Score the Fat Cap (Optional):
    - Using a sharp knife, score the fat cap in a crisscross pattern, being careful not to cut into the meat. This will help the fat render and crisp up during grilling.
3. Season the Meat:
    - Generously season the entire surface of the picanha with coarse salt. If desired, you can also season with garlic powder, black pepper, or other spices of your choice. Allow the salt to penetrate the meat for at least 30 minutes at room temperature before grilling.
4. Prepare the Grill:
    - Preheat your grill to medium-high heat (about 375-400°F or 190-200°C). If using charcoal, arrange the coals for direct grilling.
5. Grill the Picanha:
    - Once the grill is hot, place the picanha on the grill with the fat side facing up. This allows the fat to render and baste the meat as it cooks.
    - Grill the picanha for about 5-7 minutes on each side, depending on the thickness of the meat and your desired level of doneness. Use tongs to flip the meat halfway through cooking.
6. Check for Doneness:
    - The internal temperature of the picanha should reach about 130-135°F (54-57°C) for medium-rare or 140-145°F (60-63°C) for medium doneness. Use a meat thermometer inserted into the thickest part of the meat to check the temperature.
7. Rest the Meat:

- Once cooked to your liking, remove the picanha from the grill and transfer it to a cutting board. Tent it loosely with foil and let it rest for about 10 minutes. This allows the juices to redistribute and ensures a juicy and tender result.
8. Slice and Serve:
    - To serve, slice the picanha against the grain into thin slices. Serve immediately while still warm.
9. Optional Chimichurri Sauce (Traditional Argentinean Sauce):
    - If desired, serve the grilled picanha with chimichurri sauce on the side. Chimichurri is a tangy and herbaceous sauce made with parsley, garlic, olive oil, vinegar, and spices.

Enjoy the delicious flavors of Brazilian-style grilled picanha, a popular and flavorful cut of beef!

**Pisco Sour**

Ingredients:

- 2 oz (60 ml) Pisco (Peruvian grape brandy)
- 1 oz (30 ml) fresh lime juice
- 3/4 oz (22 ml) simple syrup (1:1 ratio of water to sugar)
- 1/2 oz (15 ml) pasteurized egg white (optional)
- Angostura bitters, for garnish
- Ice cubes

Instructions:

1. Prepare the Glass:
    - Chill a coupe glass or old-fashioned glass by placing it in the freezer for a few minutes before serving.
2. Shake Ingredients:
    - In a cocktail shaker, combine the Pisco, fresh lime juice, simple syrup, and pasteurized egg white (if using).
    - Fill the shaker with ice cubes.
3. Shake Vigorously:
    - Secure the lid of the cocktail shaker and shake the mixture vigorously for about 15-20 seconds. This will chill the ingredients and create a frothy texture.
4. Strain into Glass:
    - Strain the shaken mixture into the chilled glass. Use a fine-mesh strainer if you prefer to remove any ice shards or citrus pulp.
5. Garnish:
    - Garnish the Pisco Sour with a few drops of Angostura bitters on top. You can create decorative patterns or simply add a few dashes in the center.
6. Serve:
    - Serve the Pisco Sour immediately while it's cold and frothy.
7. Enjoy Responsibly:
    - Sip and enjoy the refreshing and tangy flavors of the Pisco Sour responsibly.

This classic cocktail is perfect for any occasion, whether you're relaxing at home or entertaining guests. Cheers!

**Pão de Queijo**

Ingredients:

- 2 cups (250g) tapioca flour (also known as tapioca starch)
- 1 cup (240ml) milk
- 1/2 cup (120ml) vegetable oil
- 1 teaspoon salt
- 1 1/2 cups (150g) grated Parmesan cheese or other firm cheese (such as Pecorino Romano or sharp cheddar)
- 2 eggs

Instructions:

1. Preheat the Oven:
    - Preheat your oven to 375°F (190°C). Grease a mini muffin tin or line it with paper liners.
2. Heat Milk and Oil:
    - In a saucepan, combine the milk, vegetable oil, and salt. Heat over medium heat until it starts to simmer.
3. Mix the Tapioca Flour:
    - Place the tapioca flour in a large mixing bowl. Once the milk mixture is heated, pour it over the tapioca flour.
4. Mix and Rest:
    - Stir the mixture with a wooden spoon until well combined. Let it rest for a few minutes to cool slightly.
5. Add Cheese and Eggs:
    - Add the grated Parmesan cheese to the tapioca mixture and stir until incorporated.
    - Beat the eggs lightly in a small bowl, then add them to the mixture. Stir until the eggs are fully incorporated and the dough is smooth.
6. Form the Dough Balls:
    - Using a spoon or a cookie scoop, portion out small balls of dough and place them into the prepared mini muffin tin, filling each cup about 3/4 full.
7. Bake:
    - Bake the pão de queijo in the preheated oven for about 15-20 minutes, or until they are puffed up and golden brown on top.
8. Serve Warm:
    - Remove the pão de queijo from the oven and let them cool for a few minutes before serving.

- Enjoy the warm and cheesy pão de queijo as a delicious snack or side dish.

These Brazilian cheese bread balls are best served fresh and warm, but they can also be stored in an airtight container at room temperature for a day or two. Simply reheat them in the oven or microwave before serving, if desired. Enjoy!

**Quesadillas**

Ingredients:

- 8 large flour tortillas
- 2 cups shredded cheese (such as cheddar, Monterey Jack, or a Mexican blend)
- 1 cup cooked protein (chicken, beef, shrimp, or beans)
- 1/2 cup diced bell peppers (any color)
- 1/2 cup diced onions
- 1/4 cup chopped fresh cilantro (optional)
- 2 tablespoons vegetable oil or butter, divided
- Optional toppings: salsa, sour cream, guacamole, diced tomatoes

Instructions:

1. Prepare the Fillings:
    - If using cooked protein (chicken, beef, shrimp, or beans), make sure it's cooked and seasoned to your liking.
    - Dice the bell peppers and onions. You can sauté them in a little oil until they're softened if you prefer.
2. Assemble the Quesadillas:
    - Lay out 4 tortillas on a flat surface. Sprinkle a layer of shredded cheese evenly over each tortilla.
    - Distribute the cooked protein, diced bell peppers, diced onions, and chopped cilantro (if using) evenly over the cheese.
    - Top each tortilla with another tortilla to form a sandwich.
3. Cook the Quesadillas:
    - Heat a large skillet or griddle over medium heat. Add a small amount of oil or butter to the skillet and spread it around.
    - Carefully transfer one quesadilla to the skillet and cook for 2-3 minutes on each side, or until the tortillas are golden brown and the cheese is melted.
    - Repeat with the remaining quesadillas, adding more oil or butter to the skillet as needed.
4. Serve:
    - Once cooked, remove the quesadillas from the skillet and transfer them to a cutting board.
    - Let them cool for a minute or two, then use a sharp knife to cut each quesadilla into wedges.
    - Serve the quesadillas hot with your favorite toppings, such as salsa, sour cream, guacamole, or diced tomatoes.

Enjoy these delicious and customizable quesadillas as a quick and satisfying meal or snack!

**Ropa Vieja**

Ingredients:

- 2 lbs (about 1 kg) flank steak or skirt steak
- 1 onion, finely chopped
- 1 green bell pepper, thinly sliced
- 1 red bell pepper, thinly sliced
- 3 cloves garlic, minced
- 1 can (14.5 oz) diced tomatoes
- 1 cup beef broth
- 1 tablespoon tomato paste
- 1 teaspoon ground cumin
- 1 teaspoon paprika
- 1 teaspoon dried oregano
- Salt and pepper to taste
- 2 bay leaves
- 2 tablespoons vegetable oil
- Cooked white rice, for serving
- Optional garnishes: chopped fresh cilantro or parsley, sliced green olives

Instructions:

1. Prepare the Beef:
    - Season the flank steak or skirt steak with salt and pepper on both sides.
    - Heat 1 tablespoon of vegetable oil in a large skillet or Dutch oven over medium-high heat.
    - Add the steak to the skillet and sear it on both sides until browned, about 3-4 minutes per side.
    - Transfer the seared steak to a plate and set aside.
2. Sauté Aromatics:
    - In the same skillet or Dutch oven, add the remaining tablespoon of vegetable oil.
    - Add the chopped onion, sliced bell peppers, and minced garlic to the skillet. Sauté until the vegetables are softened, about 5 minutes.
3. Simmer the Sauce:
    - Stir in the diced tomatoes, beef broth, tomato paste, ground cumin, paprika, dried oregano, salt, pepper, and bay leaves.
    - Return the seared steak to the skillet, nestling it into the sauce.
    - Bring the mixture to a simmer, then reduce the heat to low.

- Cover and let it simmer gently for 2-3 hours, or until the beef is tender and easily shreds with a fork. Stir occasionally and add more broth if needed to keep the meat moist.
4. Shred the Beef:
    - Once the beef is tender, remove it from the skillet and place it on a cutting board.
    - Use two forks to shred the beef into bite-sized pieces.
5. Return Beef to Sauce:
    - Return the shredded beef to the skillet and mix it with the sauce and vegetables.
6. Serve:
    - Serve the Ropa Vieja hot over cooked white rice.
    - Garnish with chopped fresh cilantro or parsley and sliced green olives, if desired.

Enjoy the rich and flavorful taste of Ropa Vieja, a classic Cuban dish of shredded beef simmered in a savory tomato-based sauce with bell peppers and onions!

**Sancocho**

Ingredients:

- 2 lbs (about 1 kg) chicken pieces (bone-in, skin-on)
- 1 lb (about 450 g) pork ribs or pork belly, cut into chunks
- 1 lb (about 450 g) beef stew meat, cut into chunks
- 2 ears of corn, each cut into 3-4 pieces
- 2 green plantains, peeled and cut into chunks
- 1 lb (about 450 g) yuca (cassava), peeled and cut into chunks
- 2 large carrots, peeled and cut into chunks
- 2 ripe tomatoes, diced
- 1 onion, chopped
- 4 cloves garlic, minced
- 1 bell pepper, chopped
- 1 bunch of fresh cilantro, chopped
- 1 tablespoon dried oregano
- 1 tablespoon ground cumin
- 1 tablespoon vegetable oil
- Salt and pepper to taste
- Water
- Lime wedges, for serving
- Avocado slices, for serving
- Cooked white rice, for serving

Instructions:

1. Prepare the Meat:
    - Season the chicken pieces, pork ribs or belly, and beef stew meat with salt and pepper.
    - Heat vegetable oil in a large pot or Dutch oven over medium-high heat.
    - Brown the seasoned meat in batches, then remove and set aside.
2. Sauté Aromatics:
    - In the same pot, add the chopped onion, minced garlic, and bell pepper. Sauté until softened.
    - Add the diced tomatoes, dried oregano, and ground cumin. Cook for another 2-3 minutes.
3. Simmer the Soup:
    - Return the browned meat to the pot.
    - Add enough water to cover the meat by about 2 inches.

- Bring the pot to a boil, then reduce the heat to low and let it simmer, partially covered, for about 1 hour.
4. Add Vegetables:
    - After the meat has simmered for an hour, add the chunks of corn, green plantains, yuca, and carrots to the pot.
    - Continue to simmer, partially covered, for another 30-45 minutes, or until the vegetables are tender and the meat is cooked through.
5. Adjust Seasoning:
    - Taste the sancocho and adjust the seasoning with salt and pepper as needed.
6. Serve:
    - Ladle the sancocho into bowls, making sure to include a variety of meats and vegetables in each serving.
    - Garnish with chopped fresh cilantro.
    - Serve hot with lime wedges, avocado slices, and cooked white rice on the side.

Enjoy the hearty and comforting flavors of this traditional Latin American stew! Sancocho is perfect for warming up on cold days or for sharing with family and friends.

**Seco de Pollo**

Ingredients:

- 2 lbs (about 1 kg) chicken pieces (bone-in, skin-on)
- 1/4 cup vegetable oil
- 1 large onion, finely chopped
- 4 cloves garlic, minced
- 2 tablespoons ground cumin
- 1 tablespoon ground paprika
- 1 teaspoon dried oregano
- 1 teaspoon ground black pepper
- 1/2 teaspoon ground cayenne pepper (optional, for heat)
- 2 cups chicken broth
- 2 cups beer (pilsner or lager)
- 2 tablespoons tomato paste
- 1/4 cup chopped fresh cilantro
- 2 carrots, peeled and cut into chunks
- 2 potatoes, peeled and cut into chunks
- Salt to taste
- Cooked white rice, for serving
- Sliced red onions marinated in lime juice, for garnish

Instructions:

1. Brown the Chicken:
    - Heat the vegetable oil in a large Dutch oven or heavy-bottomed pot over medium-high heat.
    - Season the chicken pieces with salt and pepper.
    - Working in batches, brown the chicken pieces on all sides until golden brown. Remove and set aside.
2. Sauté Aromatics:
    - In the same pot, add the chopped onion and minced garlic. Sauté until softened and fragrant, about 2-3 minutes.
3. Add Spices and Liquid:
    - Stir in the ground cumin, ground paprika, dried oregano, ground black pepper, and ground cayenne pepper (if using). Cook for another minute to toast the spices.
    - Deglaze the pot with the chicken broth and beer, scraping up any browned bits from the bottom of the pot.

- Stir in the tomato paste until well combined.
4. Simmer the Chicken:
    - Return the browned chicken pieces to the pot, along with any juices that have accumulated.
    - Bring the liquid to a simmer, then reduce the heat to low.
    - Cover and let the chicken simmer gently for about 30-40 minutes, or until the chicken is cooked through and tender.
5. Add Vegetables:
    - Once the chicken is cooked, add the chopped carrots and potatoes to the pot.
    - Continue to simmer, uncovered, for another 15-20 minutes, or until the vegetables are tender and the sauce has thickened.
6. Finish and Serve:
    - Stir in the chopped fresh cilantro and adjust the seasoning with salt to taste.
    - Serve the seco de pollo hot, accompanied by cooked white rice.
    - Garnish with sliced red onions marinated in lime juice for a burst of freshness and acidity.

Enjoy this flavorful and comforting Peruvian chicken stew with your favorite side dishes!

**Shrimp Tacos**

Ingredients:

- 1 lb (about 450 g) large shrimp, peeled and deveined
- 2 tablespoons olive oil
- 1 teaspoon chili powder
- 1/2 teaspoon ground cumin
- 1/2 teaspoon garlic powder
- 1/4 teaspoon smoked paprika
- Salt and pepper to taste
- 8 small flour or corn tortillas
- 1 cup shredded lettuce or cabbage
- 1 avocado, sliced
- 1/2 cup diced tomatoes
- 1/4 cup diced red onion
- 1/4 cup chopped fresh cilantro
- Lime wedges, for serving
- Optional toppings: salsa, sour cream, sliced jalapeños

Instructions:

1. Marinate the Shrimp:
    - In a mixing bowl, combine the peeled and deveined shrimp with olive oil, chili powder, ground cumin, garlic powder, smoked paprika, salt, and pepper. Toss until the shrimp are evenly coated in the seasoning mixture. Let them marinate for about 15-20 minutes.
2. Cook the Shrimp:
    - Heat a large skillet or grill pan over medium-high heat. Once hot, add the marinated shrimp to the skillet in a single layer.
    - Cook the shrimp for 2-3 minutes on each side, or until they are pink and opaque. Be careful not to overcook them, as shrimp can become rubbery if cooked for too long.
    - Once cooked, remove the shrimp from the skillet and set aside.
3. Warm the Tortillas:
    - In the same skillet or on a clean grill pan, warm the tortillas for about 30 seconds on each side, or until they are soft and pliable. You can also warm them in a microwave wrapped in a damp paper towel for 20-30 seconds.
4. Assemble the Tacos:

        - To assemble each taco, place a small handful of shredded lettuce or cabbage on a warm tortilla.
        - Top with a few cooked shrimp, sliced avocado, diced tomatoes, diced red onion, and chopped fresh cilantro.
        - Squeeze fresh lime juice over the taco for extra flavor.
        - Add any optional toppings you like, such as salsa, sour cream, or sliced jalapeños.
5. Serve:
        - Serve the shrimp tacos immediately, with lime wedges on the side for squeezing.
        - Enjoy these delicious and flavorful tacos as a light and satisfying meal!

These shrimp tacos are perfect for a quick and easy weeknight dinner or for entertaining guests at a casual gathering. Feel free to customize them with your favorite toppings and enjoy!

**Sopes**

Ingredients:

For the Sopes:

- 2 cups masa harina (corn flour)
- 1 1/4 cups warm water
- 1/2 teaspoon salt
- Vegetable oil for frying

For the Toppings (Optional):

- Refried beans
- Cooked and seasoned meat (such as shredded chicken, beef, or pork)
- Chopped lettuce or cabbage
- Diced tomatoes
- Diced onions
- Sliced jalapeños
- Crumbled queso fresco or shredded cheese
- Mexican crema or sour cream
- Salsa or hot sauce
- Chopped cilantro
- Lime wedges

Instructions:

1. Prepare the Dough:
    - In a mixing bowl, combine the masa harina and salt.
    - Gradually add the warm water to the masa harina, mixing with your hands until a soft dough forms. The dough should be pliable and not sticky. If it's too dry, add a little more water; if it's too wet, add a little more masa harina.
    - Divide the dough into small balls, each about the size of a golf ball.
2. Shape the Sopes:
    - Take one dough ball and flatten it into a thick disk, about 1/4 inch thick, using your hands. The edges should be slightly thicker than the center to form a rim.
    - Repeat with the remaining dough balls.
3. Fry the Sopes:

- Heat a skillet or griddle over medium-high heat. Lightly grease the surface with vegetable oil.
- Place the shaped sopes on the hot skillet and cook for about 2-3 minutes on each side, or until lightly golden and cooked through. You may need to work in batches.
- Once cooked, transfer the sopes to a plate lined with paper towels to drain any excess oil.

4. Assemble the Sopes:
   - Once all the sopes are cooked and drained, top each one with a spoonful of refried beans, spreading it evenly over the surface.
   - Add your choice of cooked and seasoned meat on top of the beans.
   - Garnish with chopped lettuce or cabbage, diced tomatoes, diced onions, sliced jalapeños, crumbled queso fresco or shredded cheese, Mexican crema or sour cream, salsa or hot sauce, chopped cilantro, and a squeeze of lime juice.
5. Serve:
   - Serve the sopes immediately while warm.
   - Enjoy these delicious and versatile Mexican antojitos as a snack, appetizer, or main dish!

Feel free to customize your sopes with your favorite toppings and fillings. They're perfect for showcasing a variety of flavors and textures, making them a hit at any fiesta!

## Tacos al Pastor

Ingredients:

For the Marinade:

- 3 dried guajillo chilies, stemmed and seeded
- 3 dried ancho chilies, stemmed and seeded
- 2 cloves garlic
- 1/2 small onion, chopped
- 1/4 cup pineapple juice
- 2 tablespoons white vinegar
- 1 tablespoon achiote paste
- 1 tablespoon ground cumin
- 1 tablespoon dried oregano
- 1 teaspoon smoked paprika
- 1 teaspoon salt
- 1/2 teaspoon ground black pepper

For the Tacos:

- 2 lbs (about 900 g) pork shoulder, thinly sliced
- 1/2 small pineapple, peeled and thinly sliced
- Corn tortillas
- Chopped fresh cilantro, for garnish
- Diced onions, for garnish
- Lime wedges, for serving

Instructions:

1. Prepare the Marinade:
    - In a bowl, pour boiling water over the dried guajillo and ancho chilies. Let them soak for about 15-20 minutes, until softened.
    - Drain the chilies and transfer them to a blender.
    - Add garlic, chopped onion, pineapple juice, white vinegar, achiote paste, ground cumin, dried oregano, smoked paprika, salt, and ground black pepper to the blender.
    - Blend until smooth, adding a little water if needed to achieve a thick but pourable consistency.
2. Marinate the Pork:

- Place the thinly sliced pork shoulder in a large bowl or resealable plastic bag.
- Pour the marinade over the pork, making sure it's well coated. Marinate in the refrigerator for at least 2 hours, or preferably overnight, to allow the flavors to penetrate the meat.
3. Cook the Tacos:
    - Preheat a grill or grill pan over medium-high heat.
    - Thread the marinated pork slices onto skewers, alternating with slices of pineapple.
    - Grill the skewers for about 5-7 minutes on each side, or until the pork is cooked through and slightly charred, and the pineapple is caramelized.
    - Once cooked, remove the pork and pineapple from the skewers and chop them into small pieces.
4. Assemble the Tacos:
    - Warm the corn tortillas on the grill or in a skillet.
    - Fill each tortilla with the chopped pork and pineapple mixture.
    - Garnish with chopped fresh cilantro and diced onions.
    - Serve the tacos al pastor with lime wedges on the side.
5. Serve:
    - Serve the tacos al pastor immediately while warm.
    - Enjoy these flavorful and juicy tacos as a delicious and satisfying meal!

Tacos al pastor are a classic Mexican street food favorite, known for their tender and flavorful marinated pork, caramelized pineapple, and aromatic spices. Try making them at home for an authentic taste of Mexico!

**Tamales**

Ingredients:

For the Filling:

- 2 cups shredded cooked chicken or pork
- 1 cup salsa verde or red salsa
- 1 onion, finely chopped
- 2 cloves garlic, minced
- 1 teaspoon ground cumin
- Salt and pepper to taste
- Vegetable oil for sautéing

For the Corn Dough (Masa):

- 2 cups masa harina (corn flour)
- 1 1/3 cups chicken or vegetable broth, warmed
- 2/3 cup vegetable shortening or lard
- 1 teaspoon baking powder
- 1 teaspoon salt

For Assembling:

- Dried corn husks, soaked in warm water until pliable
- Optional: Additional fillings such as sliced jalapeños, olives, or cheese

Instructions:

1. Prepare the Filling:
    - Heat a little vegetable oil in a skillet over medium heat.
    - Sauté the chopped onion and minced garlic until softened and translucent.
    - Add the shredded cooked chicken or pork to the skillet.
    - Stir in the salsa verde or red salsa, ground cumin, salt, and pepper.
    - Cook for a few minutes until heated through. Remove from heat and set aside.
2. Prepare the Corn Dough (Masa):
    - In a mixing bowl, combine the masa harina, warmed chicken or vegetable broth, vegetable shortening or lard, baking powder, and salt.
    - Mix until a soft dough forms. The dough should be pliable and easy to spread.
3. Assemble the Tamales:

- Take a soaked corn husk and pat it dry with a kitchen towel.
- Spread a thin layer of the corn dough (masa) onto the center of the husk, leaving about 1-2 inches of space at the top and bottom edges.
- Place a spoonful of the prepared filling in the center of the masa.
- If desired, add additional fillings such as sliced jalapeños, olives, or cheese on top of the filling.
- Fold the sides of the corn husk over the filling, then fold up the bottom to enclose it.
- Tie the tamale securely with kitchen twine or a strip of corn husk.

4. Steam the Tamales:
   - Arrange the assembled tamales upright in a steamer basket, open ends facing up.
   - Add water to the bottom of the steamer pot, making sure it doesn't touch the tamales.
   - Cover the pot with a lid and steam the tamales over medium heat for about 60-90 minutes, or until the masa is cooked through and firm.
   - Check the water level periodically and add more water as needed to maintain steam.

5. Serve:
   - Once cooked, carefully remove the tamales from the steamer and let them cool slightly before serving.
   - Unwrap the tamales from the corn husks and serve them warm.
   - Enjoy the delicious homemade tamales with your favorite toppings, such as salsa, sour cream, or guacamole.

These homemade tamales are perfect for sharing with family and friends on special occasions or any time you're craving authentic Mexican comfort food!

**Tostones**

Ingredients:

- 2 green (unripe) plantains
- Vegetable oil for frying
- Salt to taste
- Optional toppings: garlic sauce, mojo sauce, or your favorite dipping sauce

Instructions:

1. Peel and Cut the Plantains:
    - Start by peeling the green plantains. To do this, cut off both ends of the plantain and make a lengthwise slit along the ridges of the plantain. Carefully peel away the skin.
    - Cut the peeled plantains into slices, about 1 inch thick.
2. Fry the Plantains:
    - Heat vegetable oil in a large skillet or frying pan over medium-high heat.
    - Once the oil is hot, carefully add the plantain slices to the skillet in a single layer, making sure not to overcrowd them.
    - Fry the plantains for about 2-3 minutes on each side, or until they are golden brown and crispy.
    - Remove the fried plantains from the skillet and place them on a paper towel-lined plate to drain any excess oil.
3. Flatten the Plantains:
    - Using the bottom of a flat, heavy object (such as a glass or a plate), gently press down on each fried plantain slice to flatten it into a disc. You can also use a tostonera if you have one.
    - Press down until the plantain slice is about 1/4 inch thick.
4. Fry Again:
    - Return the flattened plantains to the hot oil and fry them for an additional 1-2 minutes on each side, or until they are golden brown and crispy.
    - Remove the tostones from the skillet and place them back on the paper towel-lined plate to drain any excess oil.
5. Season and Serve:
    - Immediately sprinkle the hot tostones with salt to taste while they are still warm.
    - Serve the tostones hot with your favorite dipping sauce, such as garlic sauce, mojo sauce, or any other dipping sauce of your choice.

Enjoy these delicious and crispy tostones as a tasty appetizer, side dish, or snack! They're perfect for dipping into your favorite sauces or enjoying on their own.

**Tortilla Soup**

Ingredients:

For the Soup:

- 6 cups chicken broth
- 1 onion, chopped
- 3 cloves garlic, minced
- 1 can (14.5 oz) diced tomatoes, undrained
- 1 can (4 oz) diced green chilies
- 1 teaspoon ground cumin
- 1 teaspoon chili powder
- Salt and pepper to taste
- 2 cups shredded cooked chicken breast
- 1 cup frozen corn kernels
- 1 can (15 oz) black beans, drained and rinsed
- Juice of 1 lime
- Chopped fresh cilantro, for garnish
- Tortilla strips or crushed tortilla chips, for garnish
- Avocado slices, for garnish
- Sour cream or Mexican crema, for garnish
- Shredded cheese, for garnish

Instructions:

1. Prepare the Soup Base:
    - In a large pot, combine the chicken broth, chopped onion, minced garlic, diced tomatoes, diced green chilies, ground cumin, and chili powder.
    - Season with salt and pepper to taste.
    - Bring the soup to a boil, then reduce the heat to low and let it simmer for about 10-15 minutes to allow the flavors to meld together.
2. Add Chicken and Vegetables:
    - Add the shredded cooked chicken breast, frozen corn kernels, and drained black beans to the pot.
    - Continue to simmer the soup for another 10-15 minutes, or until heated through and the vegetables are tender.
3. Season and Finish:
    - Stir in the lime juice to brighten the flavors.
    - Taste the soup and adjust the seasoning with salt and pepper as needed.
4. Serve:

- Ladle the hot tortilla soup into bowls.
- Garnish each bowl with chopped fresh cilantro, tortilla strips or crushed tortilla chips, avocado slices, a dollop of sour cream or Mexican crema, and shredded cheese.
- Serve the tortilla soup hot and enjoy!

This flavorful and comforting tortilla soup is perfect for warming up on chilly days or for a cozy night in. Feel free to customize the toppings to your liking and serve with warm tortillas or crusty bread for a complete meal.

**Vaca Frita**

Ingredients:

- 2 lbs flank steak or skirt steak
- 1 onion, thinly sliced
- 4 cloves garlic, minced
- 1 teaspoon ground cumin
- 1 teaspoon dried oregano
- 1 teaspoon paprika
- Salt and pepper to taste
- 2 tablespoons lime juice
- 2 tablespoons vegetable oil
- Chopped fresh cilantro, for garnish
- Lime wedges, for serving

Instructions:

1. Prepare the Steak:
    - Season the flank steak or skirt steak generously with salt and pepper on both sides.
    - In a large pot or Dutch oven, add the seasoned steak and enough water to cover it.
    - Bring the water to a boil, then reduce the heat to low and simmer for about 1 to 1 1/2 hours, or until the steak is fork-tender and easily shreds.
2. Shred the Beef:
    - Once the steak is cooked, remove it from the pot and let it cool slightly.
    - Using two forks, shred the beef into bite-sized pieces.
3. Marinate the Shredded Beef:
    - In a bowl, combine the shredded beef with minced garlic, ground cumin, dried oregano, paprika, and lime juice. Toss until the beef is evenly coated with the marinade. Let it marinate for at least 30 minutes to allow the flavors to meld.
4. Sear the Beef:
    - Heat vegetable oil in a large skillet or frying pan over medium-high heat.
    - Add the thinly sliced onion to the skillet and sauté until softened and lightly caramelized.
    - Add the marinated shredded beef to the skillet in batches, spreading it out in a single layer to ensure even browning.

- Cook the beef without stirring for a few minutes until it forms a golden crust on the bottom. Then, flip the beef and cook for a few more minutes to crisp up the other side.
5. Finish and Serve:
    - Once the beef is crispy and golden brown, remove it from the skillet and transfer it to a serving platter.
    - Garnish the vaca frita with chopped fresh cilantro and serve hot with lime wedges on the side.

Enjoy the crispy and flavorful vaca frita with rice, beans, and fried plantains for an authentic Cuban meal experience!

**Yuca Frita**

Ingredients:

- 1 large yuca root
- Vegetable oil for frying
- Salt to taste
- Optional dipping sauce: mojo sauce or garlic sauce

Instructions:

1. Prepare the Yuca:
    - Peel the yuca root using a sharp knife. Cut off both ends, then make a lengthwise slit along the skin. Carefully peel away the skin, ensuring to remove any brown spots or fibers.
    - Cut the peeled yuca into manageable-sized pieces, about 3 inches long.
2. Boil the Yuca:
    - Place the cut yuca pieces in a pot of boiling salted water. Boil for about 15-20 minutes, or until the yuca is fork-tender.
    - Drain the boiled yuca and let it cool slightly.
3. Cut and Prepare for Frying:
    - Once the boiled yuca has cooled, cut each piece lengthwise into thick fries or wedges, about 1/2 to 1 inch wide.
    - Remove any fibrous or woody cores from the center of the yuca fries.
4. Fry the Yuca:
    - Heat vegetable oil in a deep fryer or large skillet to 350°F (180°C).
    - Carefully add the yuca fries to the hot oil in batches, making sure not to overcrowd the pan.
    - Fry the yuca fries for about 4-6 minutes, or until they are golden brown and crispy on the outside.
5. Drain and Season:
    - Once the yuca fries are cooked, use a slotted spoon or spider strainer to remove them from the hot oil.
    - Place the fried yuca fries on a plate lined with paper towels to drain any excess oil.
    - Immediately sprinkle the hot yuca fries with salt to taste while they are still warm.
6. Serve:
    - Serve the yuca fries hot as a delicious appetizer or side dish.

- - Optionally, serve with a dipping sauce such as mojo sauce or garlic sauce for extra flavor.

Enjoy the crispy and flavorful yuca fries as a tasty snack or accompaniment to your favorite dishes!

## Ajiaco

Ingredients:

For the Soup:

- 2 bone-in, skin-on chicken breasts
- 2 bone-in, skin-on chicken thighs
- 8 cups chicken broth
- 1 onion, chopped
- 4 cloves garlic, minced
- 2 ears of corn, husked and cut into 2-inch pieces
- 2 large potatoes, peeled and cut into chunks
- 1 large sweet potato, peeled and cut into chunks
- 2 green plantains, peeled and cut into chunks
- 1 bunch of fresh cilantro, tied with kitchen twine
- 2 tablespoons capers
- Salt and pepper to taste

For the Aji Sauce:

- 2 green onions, chopped
- 1/4 cup fresh cilantro leaves
- 1/4 cup fresh parsley leaves
- 1/4 cup fresh mint leaves
- 1/4 cup mayonnaise
- 1 tablespoon lime juice
- 1 jalapeño pepper, seeded and chopped
- Salt and pepper to taste

Instructions:

1. Prepare the Soup:
    - In a large pot, combine the chicken breasts, chicken thighs, chicken broth, chopped onion, minced garlic, and tied bunch of cilantro.
    - Bring the pot to a boil over high heat, then reduce the heat to low and let it simmer, partially covered, for about 30 minutes, or until the chicken is cooked through and tender.
2. Shred the Chicken:
    - Once the chicken is cooked, remove it from the pot and let it cool slightly.

- Remove and discard the skin and bones from the chicken breasts and thighs.
- Shred the chicken meat into bite-sized pieces using two forks.
3. Add Vegetables:
    - Return the shredded chicken to the pot.
    - Add the pieces of corn, potatoes, sweet potatoes, and green plantains to the pot.
    - Continue to simmer the soup, uncovered, for about 20-25 minutes, or until the vegetables are tender and cooked through.
4. Season and Finish:
    - Stir in the capers and season the soup with salt and pepper to taste.
    - Remove the bunch of cilantro from the pot before serving.
5. Prepare the Aji Sauce:
    - In a blender or food processor, combine the chopped green onions, cilantro leaves, parsley leaves, mint leaves, mayonnaise, lime juice, and chopped jalapeño pepper.
    - Blend until smooth.
    - Season the aji sauce with salt and pepper to taste.
6. Serve:
    - Ladle the hot ajiaco soup into bowls.
    - Serve the soup hot, with the aji sauce on the side for drizzling over the soup.
    - Enjoy this comforting and flavorful Colombian dish!

Ajiaco is traditionally served with white rice and avocado slices on the side. You can also accompany it with a slice of ripe banana or a portion of corn on the cob.

**Birria Tacos**

Ingredients:

For the Birria:

- 3 lbs beef chuck roast or beef shank
- 1 onion, quartered
- 4 cloves garlic, minced
- 2 bay leaves
- 1 cinnamon stick
- 1 tablespoon dried oregano
- 1 tablespoon ground cumin
- 1 tablespoon smoked paprika
- 2 teaspoons salt
- 1 teaspoon black pepper
- 4 cups beef broth or water
- 2 cups canned diced tomatoes with juices
- 1/2 cup apple cider vinegar
- 2-3 dried guajillo chilies, stemmed and seeded (optional, for extra flavor and color)

For the Tacos:

- Corn tortillas
- Shredded cheese (such as Oaxaca cheese or mozzarella)
- Chopped fresh cilantro
- Diced onions
- Lime wedges
- Sliced radishes (optional, for garnish)
- Sliced jalapeños (optional, for garnish)

Instructions:

1. Prepare the Birria:
    - Trim excess fat from the beef chuck roast or beef shank, then cut it into large chunks.
    - In a large pot or Dutch oven, combine the beef chunks, quartered onion, minced garlic, bay leaves, cinnamon stick, dried oregano, ground cumin, smoked paprika, salt, black pepper, beef broth or water, canned diced

tomatoes with juices, apple cider vinegar, and dried guajillo chilies (if using).
   - Bring the mixture to a boil over high heat, then reduce the heat to low and let it simmer, partially covered, for about 3-4 hours, or until the beef is tender and falls apart easily.
2. Shred the Beef:
   - Once the beef is cooked, remove it from the pot and let it cool slightly.
   - Using two forks, shred the beef into smaller pieces. Discard any large pieces of fat or connective tissue.
3. Skim Fat and Blend Sauce (Optional):
   - If desired, skim off any excess fat from the surface of the cooking liquid.
   - Transfer the remaining cooking liquid and aromatics (onion, garlic, spices) to a blender or food processor. Blend until smooth to create a flavorful sauce.
4. Assemble the Tacos:
   - Heat a skillet or griddle over medium heat. Warm the corn tortillas on both sides until soft and pliable.
   - Fill each tortilla with a generous portion of shredded beef birria.
   - Top the birria with shredded cheese, chopped fresh cilantro, diced onions, and a squeeze of lime juice.
   - Optionally, garnish the tacos with sliced radishes and sliced jalapeños for extra flavor and heat.
5. Serve:
   - Serve the birria tacos immediately while warm.
   - Optionally, serve with a side of the blended birria sauce for dipping or drizzling over the tacos.

Enjoy these delicious and savory birria tacos, packed with tender shredded beef and flavorful spices! They're perfect for a comforting and satisfying meal any time of the day.

**Carne Asada**

Ingredients:

For the Marinade:

- 2 lbs flank steak or skirt steak
- 1/4 cup soy sauce
- 1/4 cup lime juice
- 1/4 cup orange juice
- 4 cloves garlic, minced
- 1/4 cup chopped fresh cilantro
- 2 tablespoons olive oil
- 1 teaspoon ground cumin
- 1 teaspoon chili powder
- 1 teaspoon smoked paprika
- 1 teaspoon dried oregano
- Salt and pepper to taste

For Serving:

- Corn or flour tortillas
- Chopped fresh cilantro
- Diced onions
- Sliced radishes
- Lime wedges
- Salsa or pico de gallo
- Guacamole or sliced avocado

Instructions:

1. Prepare the Marinade:
    - In a mixing bowl, combine the soy sauce, lime juice, orange juice, minced garlic, chopped fresh cilantro, olive oil, ground cumin, chili powder, smoked paprika, dried oregano, salt, and pepper. Mix well to combine.
2. Marinate the Steak:
    - Place the flank steak or skirt steak in a large resealable plastic bag or shallow dish.
    - Pour the marinade over the steak, making sure it is evenly coated.

- Seal the bag or cover the dish with plastic wrap, and refrigerate for at least 2 hours, or preferably overnight, to allow the flavors to meld and the meat to tenderize.
3. Grill the Steak:
    - Preheat your grill to medium-high heat.
    - Remove the marinated steak from the refrigerator and let it sit at room temperature for about 30 minutes before grilling.
    - Remove the steak from the marinade and discard any excess marinade.
    - Grill the steak for 4-6 minutes per side, depending on the thickness of the steak and your desired level of doneness. For medium-rare, aim for an internal temperature of 130-135°F (54-57°C).
    - Once cooked to your liking, transfer the steak to a cutting board and let it rest for 5-10 minutes before slicing.
4. Slice and Serve:
    - Slice the grilled steak across the grain into thin strips.
    - Serve the carne asada hot with warm tortillas and your choice of toppings, such as chopped fresh cilantro, diced onions, sliced radishes, lime wedges, salsa or pico de gallo, and guacamole or sliced avocado.
5. Enjoy!
    Enjoy your delicious carne asada tacos or serve it as a main dish alongside rice and beans for a flavorful meal that's perfect for any occasion!

## Chilaquiles

Ingredients:

For the Chilaquiles:

- 10 corn tortillas, cut into triangles or strips
- Vegetable oil for frying
- 2 cups red or green salsa (homemade or store-bought)
- 1 cup shredded cooked chicken or beef (optional)
- 1/2 cup crumbled queso fresco or shredded cheese
- 1/4 cup chopped fresh cilantro
- 1/4 cup diced onions
- Sour cream or Mexican crema, for serving
- Sliced avocado, for serving
- Lime wedges, for serving

Optional Toppings:

- Fried or scrambled eggs
- Sliced jalapeños
- Sliced radishes
- Sliced black olives
- Pickled onions
- Sliced green onions

Instructions:

1. Prepare the Tortillas:
    - Heat vegetable oil in a large skillet or frying pan over medium-high heat.
    - Once the oil is hot, fry the tortilla triangles or strips in batches until golden and crispy, about 1-2 minutes per side. Drain on paper towels to remove excess oil.
2. Assemble the Chilaquiles:
    - In the same skillet or a separate saucepan, heat the red or green salsa over medium heat until warmed through.
    - Add the fried tortilla chips to the salsa and toss gently to coat, allowing the chips to soften slightly.
    - If using shredded cooked chicken or beef, add it to the skillet and mix with the tortilla chips and salsa until heated through.
3. Serve:

- Transfer the chilaquiles to serving plates or a large platter.
- Sprinkle crumbled queso fresco or shredded cheese over the top.
- Garnish with chopped fresh cilantro and diced onions.
- Serve the chilaquiles hot with a dollop of sour cream or Mexican crema, sliced avocado, and lime wedges on the side.

4. Optional Toppings:
    - Top the chilaquiles with fried or scrambled eggs for added protein.
    - Add sliced jalapeños, sliced radishes, sliced black olives, pickled onions, or sliced green onions for extra flavor and texture.

5. Enjoy!
Enjoy your delicious homemade chilaquiles for breakfast, brunch, or any time of day as a satisfying and flavorful meal!

**Chupe de Camarones**

Ingredients:

- 1 lb large shrimp, peeled and deveined
- 2 tablespoons vegetable oil
- 1 onion, finely chopped
- 2 cloves garlic, minced
- 2 large tomatoes, diced
- 1 red bell pepper, diced
- 1 yellow bell pepper, diced
- 1 cup frozen corn kernels
- 1 cup frozen peas
- 4 cups seafood or chicken broth
- 1 cup heavy cream
- 1/2 cup evaporated milk
- 1/4 cup white wine (optional)
- 1/4 cup chopped fresh cilantro
- 2 tablespoons chopped fresh parsley
- 1 teaspoon ground cumin
- 1 teaspoon paprika
- Salt and pepper to taste
- 1 cup shredded mozzarella or Parmesan cheese
- 2 eggs (optional)
- Lime wedges, for serving
- Crusty bread or rice, for serving

Instructions:

1. Prepare the Shrimp:
   - If the shrimp are not already peeled and deveined, do so and then rinse them under cold water. Pat them dry with paper towels and set aside.
2. Sauté Aromatics:
   - In a large pot or Dutch oven, heat the vegetable oil over medium heat. Add the chopped onion and garlic, and sauté until softened and fragrant, about 2-3 minutes.
3. Add Vegetables:
   - Stir in the diced tomatoes, red bell pepper, and yellow bell pepper. Cook for another 5 minutes, or until the vegetables start to soften.
4. Simmer with Broth:

- Pour in the seafood or chicken broth, heavy cream, and evaporated milk. Add the white wine if using. Stir in the frozen corn kernels and peas. Bring the mixture to a simmer.
5. Season and Simmer:
    - Season the chupe with ground cumin, paprika, salt, and pepper to taste. Stir in the chopped fresh cilantro and parsley. Let the chupe simmer for 10-15 minutes to allow the flavors to meld together.
6. Add Shrimp:
    - Once the soup has simmered and the vegetables are tender, add the peeled and deveined shrimp to the pot. Cook for 3-5 minutes, or until the shrimp are pink and opaque.
7. Optional Thickening:
    - If you prefer a thicker consistency, you can whisk 2 eggs in a bowl and slowly pour them into the simmering soup while stirring constantly. Cook for an additional 2-3 minutes until the soup thickens slightly.
8. Serve:
    - Ladle the chupe de camarones into serving bowls. Sprinkle shredded mozzarella or Parmesan cheese over the top.
    - Serve hot with lime wedges on the side and crusty bread or rice for a complete meal.
9. Enjoy!

Enjoy the delicious and comforting Peruvian chupe de camarones, packed with flavorful shrimp, vegetables, and creamy broth!

**Ensalada Rusa**

Ingredients:

- 3 large potatoes, peeled and diced
- 2 carrots, peeled and diced
- 1 cup green peas, fresh or frozen
- 4 eggs
- 1 cup mayonnaise
- 2 tablespoons Dijon mustard
- 1 tablespoon white vinegar
- Salt and pepper to taste
- 1 cup cooked and diced ham (optional)
- 1/2 cup diced pickles (optional)
- 1/4 cup chopped fresh parsley, for garnish

Instructions:

1. Boil Potatoes, Carrots, and Eggs:
   - Place the diced potatoes and carrots in a pot of salted boiling water. Cook for about 10-15 minutes, or until tender but still firm.
   - In a separate pot, cover the eggs with cold water and bring to a boil. Once boiling, remove from heat, cover, and let the eggs sit in the hot water for 10-12 minutes. Then, transfer the eggs to a bowl of ice water to cool.
2. Cook Green Peas:
   - If using fresh peas, blanch them in boiling water for 2-3 minutes, then drain and rinse under cold water to stop the cooking process. If using frozen peas, thaw them under running water.
3. Prepare Dressing:
   - In a small bowl, whisk together the mayonnaise, Dijon mustard, white vinegar, salt, and pepper until well combined. Adjust seasoning to taste.
4. Assemble Salad:
   - Once the potatoes, carrots, and eggs are cooked and cooled, peel the eggs and chop them into small pieces.
   - In a large mixing bowl, combine the cooked and diced potatoes, carrots, green peas, chopped eggs, and any optional ingredients such as diced ham or pickles.
   - Pour the prepared dressing over the salad ingredients and gently toss until everything is evenly coated with the dressing.
5. Chill and Garnish:

- Cover the bowl with plastic wrap and refrigerate the ensalada rusa for at least 1-2 hours to allow the flavors to meld together and the salad to chill.
- Before serving, sprinkle chopped fresh parsley over the top for a vibrant garnish.

6. Serve:
    - Serve the ensalada rusa chilled as a refreshing side dish or appetizer for any occasion.
7. Enjoy!

Enjoy this classic and versatile ensalada rusa recipe, perfect for picnics, potlucks, or as a side dish for grilled meats and seafood!

**Pollo a la Brasa**

Ingredients:

For the Marinade:

- 1 whole chicken, about 3-4 lbs, cut into pieces (legs, thighs, wings, breasts)
- 4 cloves garlic, minced
- 2 tablespoons soy sauce
- 2 tablespoons vegetable oil
- 2 tablespoons white vinegar
- 1 tablespoon paprika
- 1 tablespoon cumin
- 1 tablespoon dried oregano
- 1 teaspoon black pepper
- Salt to taste

For Serving:

- Aji verde sauce (optional, for serving)
- French fries or roasted potatoes
- Salad or coleslaw
- Lime wedges

Instructions:

1. Prepare the Marinade:
    - In a mixing bowl, combine minced garlic, soy sauce, vegetable oil, white vinegar, paprika, cumin, dried oregano, black pepper, and salt to taste. Mix well to form a smooth marinade.
2. Marinate the Chicken:
    - Place the chicken pieces in a large resealable plastic bag or shallow dish.
    - Pour the marinade over the chicken, making sure each piece is evenly coated.
    - Seal the bag or cover the dish with plastic wrap, and refrigerate for at least 4 hours, or preferably overnight, to allow the flavors to penetrate the meat.
3. Preheat the Grill:
    - Preheat your grill to medium-high heat, about 375-400°F (190-200°C). If using a charcoal grill, prepare a two-zone fire with direct and indirect heat.
4. Grill the Chicken:

- Once the grill is hot, remove the chicken from the marinade and shake off any excess.
- Place the chicken pieces on the grill over direct heat, skin-side down. Grill for about 5-7 minutes on each side, or until the skin is golden brown and crispy, and the internal temperature reaches 165°F (74°C) for the breast meat and 175°F (80°C) for the thigh and leg meat.
- If using a charcoal grill, you may need to move the chicken to indirect heat if it starts to char too quickly.

5. Rest and Serve:
    - Once cooked through, transfer the grilled chicken pieces to a platter and let them rest for a few minutes before serving.
    - Serve the pollo a la brasa hot with aji verde sauce on the side for dipping, along with French fries or roasted potatoes, salad or coleslaw, and lime wedges for squeezing over the chicken.
6. Enjoy!
    Enjoy the delicious and flavorful pollo a la brasa, a classic Peruvian grilled chicken dish that's perfect for any occasion!

www.ingramcontent.com/pod-product-compliance
Lightning Source LLC
LaVergne TN
LVHW081603060526
838201LV00054B/2042